New Revised 3rd Edition

A Gift for Ramadhān

Shaykh Abdul Raheem Limbada
hafizahullāh

Tafseer Raheemi Publications 2024
info@tafseer-raheemi.com

A Gift for Ramadhān
3rd Edition 1st Print: February 2023 / Sha'bān 1444
3rd Edition 2nd Print: February 2024 / Rajab 1445
ISBN: 978-1-912301-16-4

Author	*Shaykh* Abdul Raheem Limbādā *Hafizahullāh* (www.tafseer-raheemi.com)
Cover Design	Ahmed Bhula
Typesetting	B.I
Printed by	Pelikan Basim, Turkey

Other available titles in this series:

A Gift for Nikāh

Available to purchase from www.tafseer-raheemi.com/shop

CONTENTS

FOREWORD

IN THE NAME OF ALLĀH ﷻ, the Most Merciful, the Most Kind. All praise is due to Allāh ﷻ who, through His infinite mercy has once again granted us another blessed Month of Ramadhān. May Allāh ﷻ accept and be pleased with us.

Alhamdulillāh, you have before you a very valuable piece of work. A detailed guide to the masā'il of Ramadhān.

Throughout the years, our honourable and respected Shaykh Abdul Raheem [Hafizahullāh] has benefitted countless people in the field of Hadīth, Tafsīr, Tasawwuf and Fiqh through lectures, courses, books and Shaykh's website www.tafseer-raheemi.com.

It was during a course in which Shaykh was teaching his compilation of 40 Hadīth relating to Ramadhān, and it was after teaching this when Shaykh decided to write a book that would act as a complete guide to Ramadhān [spiritually and practically] for one and all.

After spending many hours with Ulamā and medical doctors, you have before you a priceless book, which, Inshā-Allāh, will solve many important issues that are faced during the blessed month of Ramadhān for people young and old, in all communities across the globe.

May Allāh ﷻ accept this work and reward Shaykh Abdul Raheem [Hafizahullāh] immensely for his efforts. May Allāh ﷻ also reward the respected Muftī Shabbīr Sahib, Muftī Sūfī Tāhir Saheb, Doctor Mazharuddin Sahib, Doctor Salīm, Doctor Liāqat and Maulānā Zayd Mehtar for their contributions to this valuable piece.

May Allāh ﷻ guide us and protect us all. Āmīn

Ahmed Bhula
General Manager of www.tafseer-raheemi.com
Ramadhān 1436 AH

INTRODUCTION

Allāh ﷻ has introduced the month of Ramadhān in the Holy Qur'ān with the following verse:

شَهْرُ رَمَضَانَ الَّذِيْٓ اُنْزِلَ فِيْهِ الْقُرْاٰنُ هُدًى لِّلنَّاسِ وَبَيِّنٰتٍ مِّنَ الْهُدٰى وَالْفُرْقَانِ ج
فَمَنْ شَهِدَ مِنْكُمُ الشَّهْرَ فَلْيَصُمْهُ ط وَمَنْ كَانَ مَرِيْضًا اَوْ عَلٰى سَفَرٍ فَعِدَّةٌ مِّنْ اَيَّامٍ
اُخَرَ ط يُرِيْدُ اللهُ بِكُمُ الْيُسْرَ وَلَا يُرِيْدُ بِكُمُ الْعُسْرَ ز وَلِتُكْمِلُوا الْعِدَّةَ وَلِتُكَبِّرُوا اللهَ
عَلٰى مَا هَدٰكُمْ وَلَعَلَّكُمْ تَشْكُرُوْنَ ۝

"The month of Ramadhān is the month in which the Qur'ān was revealed as a guidance for mankind, whose verses of guidance are absolutely clear, and a criterion. So whoever among you witnesses this month, should fast in it. While those who are ill or on a journey should make up for the same number of days at another time. Allāh wants ease for you and does not want hardship for you. You should complete the period and then glorify Allāh that He guided you. And you will perhaps show gratitude to Him." [1]

The verse indicates towards the greatness of this month by saying that the greatest of all divine scriptures, the glorious Qur'ān, was revealed in this blessed month.

This revelation is of two types:

[1] Revelation from Lawhe Mahfooz to the earthly heaven took place in this month in the night of power.

[2] The beginning of revelation upon the heart of the Prophet ﷺ. The first five verses of Sūrah Alaq were revealed in the cave of Hira, in Laylatul Qadr, in this month.

[1] Qur'ān 2:185.

The Qur'ān came like a heavy rainfall in a hot climate with extreme drought. The world was dry, filled with Kufr, Shirk and disobedience. The Qur'ān came like a heavy rainfall which cools everything down and breathes life into dry lands. It had everything that was needed; guidance, clear proofs, the power to distinguish between truth and false. It breathed life into dead souls.

Since this month holds great virtues, people should fast in it. This fasting is only from dawn till dusk, and only for one month. We can eat and drink freely for eleven months, but we should bring our desires under control for just one month. There is flexibility for the sick and the travellers. This is because Allāh ﷻ is extremely kind and merciful. He does not like putting his creation in difficulties, so he granted flexibility. Allāh ﷻ wants us to complete this period and be grateful to Him for guiding us towards that which benefits us.

People should be grateful and keep fasts properly. We see that in this day and age people miss fasts or break them for silly excuses. There is an environment of godlessness out there. No wonder we suffer from individual misfortunes and collective problems around the world. May Allāh ﷻ guide us.

Some people say summer fasts are too long. However, they fail to realise that the extra effort will bring extra reward and on top of that, the pleasure of Allāh ﷻ, which is our aim.

Rasūlullāh ﷺ would sometimes fast while travelling through the desert, enduring the heat and thirst. The Sahābā رضي الله عنهم loved fasting in the hot summer days. They literally felt *lazzat* in their hardship. That is the inner pleasure, the pleasure of the soul and mind, which we so much crave.

Our *salaf* used to love it also. Maulānā Arshad Madani Saheb mentioned that his father Hadhrat Maulānā Hussain Ahmed Madani رحمه الله would be fasting in the hot summer days. He would be reciting the Qur'ān to someone after Asr Salāh. His tongue would get stuck and he would struggle to continue. He would get up and go to the *Wudhū* area, pour two jugs of water over his head and come back and continue reading. There was no air conditioning nor any fans in those days.

This book which you have in your hands was written with the intention to make *masā'il* of *Sawm* easy for everyone. We compiled *40 Hadīth* at the beginning, in order to give some encouragement to the readers. Maybe if one person observes fasts properly, this can be a source of salvation for myself and for all our Tafseer Raheemi team. This has been a collective effort rather than an individual one.

I would like to express my gratitude to Allāh ﷻ for giving me the tawfeeq to compile this book, and then I would like to thank the authors of the books I have benefited from, mainly *'Tuhfae Ramadhān'* by Muftī Salmān Mansūrpūrī. I should also mention and thank my dearest Muftī Zaid Mehtar who was the main driving force behind this. And then our Tafseer Raheemi manager Ahmed Bhula. Also Yahya Batha, Esa Bhai and the rest of the team.

May Allāh ﷻ reward each and every one of them with the best of rewards in *Dunya* and *Akhirah*. Āmīn

Shaykh Abdul Raheem Limbādā *Hafizahullāh*
16 May 2016 / 9 Sha'bān 1437

Alhamdulillah, by the Grace of Almighty Allāh ﷻ, A Gift for Ramadhān has proven popular and has been well received. It has sold out several times and we can now announce the 3rd Revised Edition of the book.

The new edition includes additional essays to aid in navigating through the blessed month, including a special treatise on Zakāt written by Muftī Mohammed Wahaajuddin of Detroit, USA, that covers some key contemporary Masā'il such as Zakāt on Cryptocurrency. Insha'Allāh, it will be of great benefit to the reader.

I would like to thank all those who participated in publishing the latest edition, including my sister, Saleha Apa, for her extremely valuable input, and Mufti Wahaajuddin for his section on Zakāt. I would also like to thank my friends Ahmed Bhula, Maulānā Belal Isakjee, and the rest of the team for their hard work and tireless efforts in getting this work published.

May Allāh ﷻ accept this work and benefit the Muslim Ummah through it, and May Allāh ﷻ be pleased with us all. Āmīn

Shaykh Abdul Raheem Limbādā *Hafizahullāh*
[Currently in] Masjid-e-Nabawi Shareef, Madinah Al-Munawarrah
31st December 2022 / 7 Jumāda Al-Thāniyah 1444

40 HADĪTH

[1] RASŪLULLĀH ﷺ PAYING GREAT IMPORTANCE TO RAMADHĀN

عن سلمان الفارسي، قال: خطبنا رسول الله صلى الله عليه وسلم في آخر يوم من شعبان فقال أيها الناس قد أظلكم شهر عظيم شهر مبارك شهر فيه ليلة خير من ألف شهر جعل الله صيامه فريضة وقيام ليله تطوعا من تقرب فيه بخصلة من الخير كان كمن أدى فريضة فيما سواه ومن أدى فيه فريضة كان كمن أدى سبعين فريضة فيما سواه وهو شهر الصبر والصبر ثوابه الجنة وشهر المواساة وشهر يزداد فيه رزق المؤمن من فطر فيه صائما كان مغفرة لذنوبه وعتق رقبته من النار وكان له مثل أجره من غير ان ينتقص من أجره شيء قالوا ليس كلنا نجد ما يفطر الصائم فقال يعطي الله هذا الثواب من فطر صائما على تمرة أو شربة ماء أو مذقة لبن وهو شهر أوله رحمة واوسطه مغفرة وآخره عتق من النار من خفف عن مملوكه غفر الله له واعتقه من النار واستكثروا فيه من أربع خصال خصلتين ترضون بهما ربكم وخصلتين لا غنى بكم عنهما فأما الخصلتان اللتان ترضون بهما ربكم فشهادة أن لا إله إلا الله وتستغفرونه وأما اللتان لاغنى بكم عنها فتسألون الله الجنة وتعوذون به من النار ومن أشبع فيه صائما سقاه الله من حوضي شربة لا يظمأ حتى يدخل الجنة ». رواه ابن خزيمة في صحيحه .

Hadhrat Salmān ﷺ reports "On the last day of Sha'bān, Allāh's Messenger ﷺ addressed us and said: 'O people, there comes over you now a great month, a most blessed month in which lies a night more greater in virtue than one thousand months. It is a month in which Allāh (The Glorified and the Exalted) has made compulsory that the days should be observed by fasting. And he has made optional the standing by night. Whosoever makes an attempt to draw nearer to Allāh ﷻ by performing any virtuous deed, for him shall be the reward like one who had performed fardh at any other time. And whoever performs fardh, for him shall be the reward of seventy fardh in any other time. This is indeed the month of patience, and the reward for true patience is Paradise. It is the month of sympathy with one's fellowmen. It is the month wherein a true believer's rizq (sustenance) is increased. Whosoever feeds another who fasted, in order to break the fast (at sunset), for him shall be forgiveness for his sins and emancipation from the fire of Hell and for him shall be the same reward as for him (who he fed) without that person's reward being decreased in the least.

Thereupon we said: "O Messenger of Allāh, not all of us possess the means whereby we can help a fasting person to break his fast." The Messenger of Allāh replied: 'Allāh grants the same reward to him who gives a fasting person, to break the fast, a mere date or a drink of water or a sip of milk. This is a month, the first part of which brings Allāh's Mercy, the middle of which brings His forgiveness and the last of which brings emancipation from the fire of Hell. Whosoever lessens the burden of His servants (labourers) in this month, Allāh (The Glorified and the Exalted) will forgive him and free him from the fire of Hell. And in this month, four things you should continue to perform in great number, two of which shall be to please your Rabb while the other two shall be those without which you cannot do. Those which shall be to please your Rabb, are that you should, abundantly, bear witness that there is no deity to worship except Allāh (i.e. recite the Kalima Tayyibah: La Ilaaha Illallah abundantly) and make much Istighfār (beg Allāh's forgiveness with Astaghfirullāh). And as for those without which you cannot do, you should beg of Allāh entrance into

Paradise and seek refuge in Him from Hell." And whoever satiated a person with food, Allāh (The Glorified and the Exalted) will give him water from the Hawdh (pond) where after he shall never again feel thirsty until he enters Paradise." [2]

[2] FASTING IS A PILLAR OF ISLAM

قال رسول الله صلى الله عليه وسلم بني الإسلام على خمس : شهادة أن لا إله إلا الله وأن محمدا رسول الله ، واقام الصلاة ، وايتاء الزكاة ، والحج ، وصوم رمضان. اخرجه البخاري ـ

"Islam is based on five pillars: To bear witness that there is none worthy of worship except Allāh and that Muhammad is Allāh's Messenger, to establish Salāh, to give Zakāt, to perform Hajj and to Fast in Ramadhān." [3]

[3] RAMADHAN EXPIATES SINS

عن أبي هريرة أن رسول الله صلى الله عليه وسلم كان يقول الصلوات الخمس والجمعة إلى الجمعة ورمضان إلى رمضان مكفرات ما بينهن إذا اجتنب الكبائر رواه مسلم ـ

Abū Hurairah ﷺ narrates that Rasūlullāh ﷺ said, "The five daily prayers, and one Jumu'ah to another Jumu'ah, and one Ramadhān to another Ramadhān, expiate the sins in between as long as one refrains from major sins." [4]

---

[2] Ibn Khuzaimah.

[3] Bukhārī.

[4] Muslim.

[4] IN RAMADHAN, THE GATES OF JANNAH ARE OPENED AND THE GATES OF JAHANNAM ARE CLOSED

عن أبي هريرة رضي الله عنه أن رسول الله صلى الله عليه وسلم قال: إذا جاء رمضان فُتّحت أبواب الجنة، وغُلّقت أبواب النار، وصُفّدت الشياطين. رواه مسلم ـ

Abū Hurairah ﷺ narrates that Rasūlullāh ﷺ said, "When the month of Ramadhān commences, the doors of the heavens are opened, the doors of Jahannam are closed, and the Shayateen are chained." [5]

This results in lessening of sins due to the reasons of sins being minimized. When the gates of Jannah are opened, it's cool breeze reaches the hearts of the believers and urges them to increase their devotion.

[5] FASTING SHOULD BE WITH BELIEF AND SINCERITY

عن أبي هريرة رضي الله عنه قال: قال رسول الله صلى الله عليه وسلم: من صام رمضان إيماناً واحتساباً ، غُفر له ما تقدم من ذنبه. رواه الشيخان ـ

Abu Hurairah ﷺ narrates that Rasūlullāh ﷺ said "Whosoever fast in Ramadhān with firm belief and with hope of gaining reward (sincerity), his previous sins will be forgiven." [6]

[5] Muslim.

[6] Bukhārī, Muslim.

[6] FIVE GREAT GIFTS FOR A SAAIM

عن أبي هريرة قال قال رسول الله صلى الله عليه وسلم : أعطيت أمتي خمس خصال في رمضان لم تعطها أمة قبلهم خلوف فم الصائم أطيب عند الله من ريح المسك وتستغفر لهم الملائكة حتى يفطروا ويزين الله عز وجل كل يوم جنته ثم يقول يوشك عبادي الصالحون ان يلقوا عنهم المؤنة والأذى ويصيروا إليك ويصفد فيه مردة الشياطين فلا يخلصوا إلى ما كانوا يخلصون إليه في غيره ويغفر لهم في آخر ليلة قيل يا رسول الله أهي ليلة القدر قال لا ولكن العامل إنما يوفى أجره إذا قضى عمله. رواه احمد ـ

Abu Hurairah ﷺ relates that Rasūlullāh ﷺ said, "My Ummah has been given five things for Ramadhān which were not given to anyone except them. For them:

[1] The khuloof of a saaim (smell exiting from the mouth due to emptiness of the stomach) is sweeter to Allāh ﷻ than the fragrant smell of musk. (i.e. Allāh ﷻ loves the saaim due to his sacrifice).

[2] The Angels seek forgiveness for the fasting person until they break their fast. [Due to their love for the Saaimeen].

[3] Allāh ﷻ decorates Jannah every day and then says, "The time is near when My faithful servants shall cast aside the great trials of the world and come to you."

[4] In this month the rebellious, giant Satans are chained so that they cannot reach unto those evils to which they normally reached during other months besides Ramadhān.

[5] On the last night of Ramadhān people are forgiven". The Sahābāh ﷺ thereupon enquired, "0 Messenger of Allāh, is that last night Laylatul Qadr? Rasūlullāh ﷺ replied, "No. But a labourer is paid his wage in full, when he completes the work. " [7]

[7] THE REWARD OF SAWM WILL BE BEYOND IMAGINATION

عن أبي هريرة رضي الله عنه عن النبي صلى الله عليه وسلم قال : « كل عمل ابن آدم يضاعف، الحسنة عشرة أمثالها إلى سبعمائة ضعف قال الله عز وجل : إلا الصوم فإنه لي وأنا أجزي به، يدع شهوته وطعامه من أجلي، للصائم فرحتان: فرحة عند فطره وفرحة عند لقاء ربه، ولخلوف فيه أطيب عند الله من ريح المسك » رواه مسلم ـ

Abu Hurairah ﷺ relates that Rasūlullāh ﷺ said, "Every deed of the son of Ādam, brings 10 hasanāt/rewards and it can be increased up to 700.

(However), Allāh says, 'Except for fast, because fasting is for Me, and I shall reward it. The Saaim leaves his desires and food for My sake.' For a fasting person there are two joys:

[1] A joy at the time of Iftaar.

[2] And a joy when he meets his Lord. The khuloof of a fasting person is more beloved to Allāh than the fragrance of musk. [8]

---

[7] Ahmed.

[8] Muslim.

This means that the rewards of general deeds will be distributed, through the angels. However, fasting is so beloved to Allāh ﷻ, that He himself will personally give its reward. When Allāh ﷻ is generous and he has no fear of poverty, imagine how much He will give.

[8] ABUNDANCE OF RAHMAH FOR THE SAAIMEEN

عن عبادة بن صامت قال قال رسول الله صلي الله عليه و سلم أتاكم رمضان شهر بركة يغشاكم الله فيه فينزل الرحمة ويحط الخطايا ويستجيب فيه الدعاء وينظر الله تعالى الى تنافسكم ويباهي بكم ملائكته فأروا الله تعالى من أنفسكم خيرا فإن الشقي من حرم فيه رحمة الله عزوجل رواه ـ

Ubādah bin Sāmit ؓ relates that Rasūlullāh ﷺ said "Ramadhān, the month of blessings has come upon you, wherein Allāh turns towards you and sends down His special mercy, He forgives your sins and accepts duās. He observes you're competing with one another in doing good deeds and He boasts to the angels about you. So show to Allāh your righteousness for verily, the most pitiable and unfortunate one is he who is deprived of Allāh's mercy, even in this month.

[9] DUĀS OF A SAAIM ARE ACCEPTED

عن ابي هريرة قال قال رسول الله صلي الله عليه و سلم ثلاثة لا ترد دعوتهم : الصائم حتى يفطر ، والإمام العادل ، ودعوة المظلوم يرفعها الله فوق الغمام ، ويفتح لها أبواب السماء ويقول الرب : وعزتي لأنصرنك ولو بعد حين. رواه الترمذي ـ

Abu Hurairah ﷺ relates that Rasūlullāh ﷺ said: "Three types of people whose supplications are not rejected:

[1] A Fasting person until he opens his fast.

[2] A just ruler.

[3] Duā of a person who is oppressed. Allāh lifts it up to the heavens and the doors of heaven are opened and Allāh says "By My honour! I will indeed help you even though it could be after a while." [9]

[10] TAWFEEQ OF KHAYR IN RAMADHĀN

عَنْ أَبِيْ هُرَيْرَةَ قَالَ : قَالَ رَسُوْلُ اللهِ صَلَّى اللهُ عَلَيْهِ وَسَلَّمَ : " إِذَا كَانَ أَوَّلُ لَيْلَةٍ مِنْ شَهْرِ رَمَضَانَ صُفِّدَتِ الشَّيَاطِيْنُ، وَمَرَدَةُ الجِنِّ، وَغُلِّقَتْ أَبْوَابُ النَّارِ، فَلَمْ يُفْتَحْ مِنْهَا بَابٌ، وَفُتِّحَتْ أَبْوَابُ الجَنَّةِ، فَلَمْ يُغْلَقْ مِنْهَا بَابٌ، وَيُنَادِيْ مُنَادٍ : يَا بَاغِيَ الخَيْرِ أَقْبِلْ، وَيَا بَاغِيَ الشَّرِّ أَقْصِرْ، وَلِلّٰهِ عُتَقَاءُ مِنَ النَّارِ، وَذٰلِكَ كُلَّ لَيْلَةٍ -

When it is the first night of Ramadhān, the Satans and the rogue Jinns are chained. The doors of Jahannam are locked, none of them are opened. The doors of Jannah are opened, none of them are closed. And an announcer announces: "O seeker of good! Proceed! And O seeker of evil! Stop!" And Allāh emancipates people from the fire, and this takes place every night." [10]

The whole Hadīth explains that the Tawfeeq of Khayr (the ability to do good deeds) is increased in Ramadhān, whereas the channels of evil are reduced during this holy month.

---

[9] Tirmīdhī.

[10] Tirmīdhī, Ibn Mājah, Mishkāt Pg.173.

[11] NIGHT PRAYER OF RAMADHĀN BRINGS FORGIVENESS

عن أبي هريرة رضي الله عنه أن رسول الله صلى الله عليه وسلم قال:

من قام رمضان إيماناً واحتساباً غُفر له ما تقدم من ذنبه متفق عليه ـ

Abū Hurairah ﵁ narrates that Rasūlullāh ﷺ said: "Whosoever stands (in prayer) in Ramadhān with firm belief and with hope of gaining reward, his previous sins will be forgiven." [11]

The indication is towards Tarāwīh Salāh. One should perform it with utmost willingness, show some desire.

[12] STANDING FOR SALAH IN LAYLATUL QADR ATTRACTS FORGIVENESS

عن أبي هريرة رضي الله عنه عن النبي صلى الله عليه وسلم قال:

من قام ليلة القدر إيماناً واحتساباً ، غُفر له ما تقدم من ذنبه متفق عليه ـ

Abū Hurairah ﵁ narrates that Rasūlullāh ﷺ said "Whosoever stands (for worship) in Laylatul Qadr (the night of power) with firm belief and with hope of gaining reward, his previous sins will be forgiven." [12]

Note: Laylatul Qadr can be any night from the last 10 nights, most likely one of the odd ones. (21st, 23rd, 25th, 27th and 29th). One should try and stay awake on these nights and perform some kind of worship.

---

[11] Bukhārī, Muslim.

[12] Bukhārī, Muslim.

[13] FASTING EXPIATES SINS

عن حذيفة بن اليمان رضي الله عنه قال: قال رسول الله صلى الله عليه وسلم: فتنة الرجل في أهله وماله وولده وجاره، تكّفرها الصلاة، والصوم، والصدقة، والأمر والنهي متفق عليه ـ

Huzaifah ﷺ narrates that Rasūlullāh ﷺ said: "The tests a man faces in his family, wealth, children and neighbours are expiated by Salāh, Sawm, Sadaqah and by calling towards good and forbidding from evil." [13]

Note: These tests can be the minor sins committed due to pressure from family and children, or due to earning and spending wealth without due care, or due to some differences with one's neighbours. Since they are not major things, they can be pardoned due to fasting and the good deeds mentioned.

[14] NOTHING CAN MATCH SAWM

عن أبي أمامة رضي الله عنه قال: أتيت رسول الله صلى الله عليه وسلم فقلت: مرني بأمر آخذه عنك، فقال: عليك بالصوم، فإنه لا مثل له. رواه النسائي ـ

"Abu Umāmah ﷺ says: I came to Rasūlullāh ﷺ and requested him to give me some advice to which I can hold on. He replied: "Hold on to Sawm, because it has no similitude." [14]

Note: Fasting is a special act of worship. One Hadīth says: "Everything has a door, and the door of worship is fasting." The author of Hidāyah wrote the book in eleven [11] years. He wrote the book whilst fasting all the time, and in such a way that not even his family knew that he was fasting. He would

---

[13] Bukhārī, Muslim.

[14] Nasa'ī.

take a tiffin from home and return with it empty. He would call some poor person in the afternoon and feed it to him.

[15] SAWM PROTECTS FROM THE FIRE

عن عثمان بن عفان رضي الله عنه، قال: سمعت رسول الله صلى الله عليه وسلم يقول: الصيام جُنّة من النار، كجنّة أحدكم من القتال. رواه ابن ماجه.

Uthmān ﷺ says I heard Rasūlullāh ﷺ saying: "Fasting is a protective shield from the fire, just like one of you has a shield to protect him in the battle." [15]

[16] AR-RAYYAAN; A SPECIAL GATE OF JANNAH FOR SAAIMEEN

عن سهل بن سعد رضي الله عنه أن النبي صلى الله عليه وسلم قال: في الجنّة ثمانية أبواب، فيها باب يُسمى الريّان، لا يدخله إلا الصائمون. رواه البخاري، وزاد النسائي: فإذا دخل آخرهم أغُلق، من دخل فيه شرب، ومن شرب لم يظمأ أبداً.

Sahl bin Sạ'd ﷺ narrates that Rasūlullāh ﷺ said: "In Jannah there is a gate called Ar-Rayyān, only the Sā'imūn (people of fasting) will enter it. [16] And in the narration of Nasa'ī there is an addition: When the last person enters, it will be closed, whosoever enters from it, will be given a drink and whomsoever drinks it, will never be thirsty again.

[15] Ibn Mājah.

[16] Bukhārī.

Note: Sā'imūn here means those who loved fasting and who used to keep a lot of voluntary fasts.

[17] BEING INVITED FROM ALL GATES

عن أبي هريرة رضي الله عنه أن رسول الله صلى الله عليه وسلم قال من أنفق زوجين في سبيل الله نودي من أبواب الجنة يا عبد الله هذا خير فمن كان من أهل الصلاة دعي من باب الصلاة ومن كان من أهل الجهاد دعي من باب الجهاد ومن كان من أهل الصيام دعي من باب الريان ومن كان من أهل الصدقة دعي من باب الصدقة فقال أبو بكر رضي الله عنه بأبي أنت وأمي يا رسول الله ما على من دعي من تلك الأبواب من ضرورة فهل يدعى أحد من تلك الأبواب كلها قال نعم وأرجو أن تكون منهم رواه البخاري ـ

Abū Hurairah ﷺ narrates that Rasūlullāh ﷺ said: "Whoever spends a pair (of clothes, shoes, or is charitable to double people etc), in the cause of Allāh will be called from the gates of Jannah: "O Abdullāh, this gate is good for you." The people of Salāh will be called from the gate of Salāh, the people of Jihād will be called from the gate of Jihād, the people of Sadaqah will be called from the gate of Sadaqah, and the people of fasting will be called from the gate of Rayyān."

Abu Bakr ﷺ said, "There is no harm on one who will be called from all these gates. So will there be anyone who would be called from all gates?" The Messenger of Allāh ﷺ said, "Yes, and I have great hope that you will be one of them." [17]

[17] Bukhārī.

Note: This is because Siddique Akbar ﷺ used to perform all these acts of worship, so he will be called from all the gates. One Hadīth states that Rasūlullāh ﷺ asked a gathering of companions: "Who is fasting today?" Abū Bakr raised his finger. He asked: "Who fed a destitute today?" Abū Bakr raised his finger to say: "I did." He asked: "Who visited a sick person today?" Abū Bakr raised his finger. He asked: "Who attended a funeral today?" Abū Bakr raised his finger. He ﷺ said: "Never do these gather in a person but he will definitely enter Jannah."

It is possible that Rasūlullāh ﷺ had a presentiment [*Kashf*] in which he realised that Siddique Akbar ﷺ had performed these acts of virtue. He wanted to inform the congregation of the greatness of Siddique Akbar ﷺ so he ﷺ asked these questions.

[18] SPECIAL SEE THROUGH MANSIONS IN JANNAH FOR PEOPLE WHO HAVE FOUR QUALITIES; ONE OF THEM IS SIYAAM

عن علي بن أبي طالب رضي الله عنه قال: قال رسول الله صلى الله عليه وسلم: إن في الجنة غرفاً تُرى ظهورها من بطونها، وبطونها من ظهورها فقام أعرابي فقال: لمن هي يا رسول الله؟ قال: لمن أطاب الكلام، وأطعم الطعام، وأدام الصيام، وصلى لله بالليل والناس نيام رواه الترمذي ـ

Alī bin Abī Tālib ﷺ narrates that Rasūlullāh ﷺ said: "In Paradise there are such rooms that their interior can be seen from outside and outside can be seen from inside. Allāh has prepared them for those who soften their speech, feed people, continuously observe fasts, and perform Salāh at night while people are asleep. [18]

[18] Tirmīdhī.

[19] INTERCESSION OF QUR'ĀN AND SIYAAM

عن عبد الله بن عمرو رضي الله عنه أن رسول الله صلى الله عليه وسلم قال: الصيام والقرآن يشفعان للعبد يوم القيامة، يقول الصيام: أي رب، منعته الطعام والشهوات بالنهار، فشفعني فيه، ويقول القرآن: منعته النوم بالليل، فشفعني فيه، فيشفعان رواه أحمد ـ

Abdullāh bin Amr ﷺ narrates that Rasūlullāh ﷺ said: "The fast and Qur'ān will intercede on behalf of the slave, on the Day of Judgement. The fast will say: "Yā Rabb! I prevented him from eating, drinking, and fulfilling his lawful desires during the day, therefore accept my intercession. Qur'ān will say: Yā Rabb! I prevented him from sleeping at night. So accept my intercession. Both the intercessions will be accepted." [19]

Note: No one will be allowed to speak up for anyone on the day of Qiyāmah except with Allāh's permission. So if someone comes forward and puts in a word for us, imagine how much happiness this will bring us.

[20] EATING SUHOOR UP TO SUBHE SADIQ

عن سهل بن سعد، قال أنزلت {وكلوا واشربوا حتى يتبين لكم الخيط الأبيض من الخيط الأسود }ولم ينزل من الفجر، فكان رجال إذا أرادوا الصوم ربط أحدهم في رجله الخيط الأبيض والخيط الأسود، ولم يزل يأكل حتى يتبين له رؤيتهما، فأنزل الله بعد {من الفجر} فعلموا أنه إنما يعني الليل والنهار رواه البخاري ـ

---

[19] Ahmed.

Sahl bin Sạ'd ﷺ narrates: When the following verses were revealed: 'Eat and drink until the white thread appears to you distinctly from the black thread', and من الفجر (from the dawn) was not yet revealed, some people who intended to fast, tied black and white threads to their feet and went on eating until (there was enough light that) they differentiated between the two. Allāh then revealed the words, 'of dawn', and it became clear that He meant night and day." [20]

i.e Suhoor should be finished by Subhe Sādiq. Onẹ cannot eat after that.

Subhe Sādiq means 'True Dawn'. One should be careful in finishing Suhoor a few minutes earlier than what is in the timetable. This is to avoid any risk of overstepping the limit.

[21] EATING SUHOOR IS DESIRABLE

عن أنس بن مالك رضي الله عنه قال: قال النبي صلى الله عليه وسلم:

تسحَّروا فإن في السحور بركة أخرجه البخاري ـ

Anas ibn Mālik ﷺ narrates that Rasūlullāh ﷺ said: "Partake from the Suhoor/pre-dawn meal, because verily there is Barakah (blessings) in Suhoor." [21]

Note: Why miss out on barkatī food? Especially when we are going to need a lot of energy throughout the day. We should make a habit of eating suhoor.

[22] SUHOOR IS A DEFINING ACT

عن عمرو بن العاص رضي الله عنه أن رسول الله صلى الله عليه وسلم قال:

[20] Bukhārī.

[21] Bukhārī.

فصل ما بين صيامنا وصيام أهل الكتاب أكلة السحر رواه مسلم ـ

Amr bin Āāṣ ﷺ narrates that Rasūlullāh ﷺ said, "The difference between our fasting and the fasting of Ahle Kitab, is the eating of Suhoor." [22]

Note: Ahle Kitab means 'people of the book' i.e. the Jews and the Christians. They used to fast as well, but they would not get up to eat anything for Suhoor. They would just eat something before going to sleep at night.

[23] ALLĀH AND HIS ANGELS SHOWER MERCY UPON SUHOOR TAKERS

عن عبد الله بن عمر رضي الله عنهما قال: قال رسول الله صلى الله عليه وسلم:

إن الله وملائكته يصلّون على المتسحّرين رواه ابن حبّان ـ

Abdullāh bin Umar ﷺ narrates that Rasūlullāh ﷺ said, "Indeed Allāh and His angels send mercy upon those who partake of Suhoor." [23]

Note: When we get up for suhoor, we should pray a few rak'āts of Tahajjud, do some Dhikr, read some Qur'ān and make some duās as well. All this attracts Allāh's ﷻ Rahmah.

[24] SUHOOR FOOD IS BARKATI FOOD

عن المقدام بن معد يكرب رضي الله عنه أن النبي صلى الله عليه وسلم قال:

عليكم بغداء السحور؛ فإنه هو الغداء المبارك رواه النسائي ـ

[22] Muslim.

[23] Ibn Ḥibbān.

Miqdam bin Made-Karab ﵁ narrates that Rasūlullāh ﷺ said, "It is imperative that you have Suhoor food, because it is indeed a blessed meal." [24]

[25] SUHOOR SHOULD BE DELAYED UP TO THE PERMITTED TIME

عن أبي الدرداء رضي الله عنه قال: قال رسول الله صلى الله عليه وسلم: ثلاث من أخلاق النبوة : تعجيل الإفطار، وتأخير السحور، ووضع اليمين على الشمال في الصلاة رواه الطبراني ـ

Abū Dardā ﵁ narrates that Rasūlullāh ﷺ said, "Three things are from the characteristics of Prophethood:

[1] To hasten in Iftaar,

[2] To delay Suhoor and,

[3] To place the right hand on the left hand in Salah." [25]

Some people do Suhoor about two hours before Subhe Sadiq. This is not Taqwā, as it goes against the Sunnah of Rasūlullāh ﷺ.

[26] TAKING A SIP OF WATER CAN BE CONSIDERED AS SUHOOR

عن عبد الله بن عمر رضي الله عنهما قال: قال رسول الله صلى الله عليه وسلم:

[24] Nasa'ī.

[25] Tabrānī.

تسحّروا ولو بجرعة من ماء رواه ابن حبّان ـ

Abdullāh bin Umar ﷺ narrates that Rasūlullāh ﷺ said: "Partake of Suhoor even though it may be a sip of water." [26]

Note: Sometimes our alarms don't go off and we get up at the last minute. We feel there is no time for suhoor, so we go back to sleep thinking we will get up later towards the end of fajr time, pray fajr and go to work. This is not right. We should at least drink a glass of water to take the Barakah of suhoor.

[27] LADIES SHOULD MAKE UP FOR THE FASTS MISSED DUE TO PERIOD

عن عائشة رضي الله عنها قالت كان يكون علي الصوم من

رمضان ، فما أستطيع أن أقضي إلا في شعبان رواه البخاري ـ

Ā'ishā ﷺ says: "Sometimes some fasts of Ramadhān would be due upon me, but I could not make up for them (qadhā) except in the month of Sha'bān. [27]

Note: This is because Rasūlullāh ﷺ would fast abundantly in the month of Sha'bān. Hadhrat Ā'ishā ﷺ says in another Hadīth that Rasūlullāh ﷺ would fast most of Sha'bān, in fact all of Sha'ban. So she would also join him and do her qadhā. We should at least fast on the 15th of Sha'bān and a few days before or after.

[28] INCREASING GENEROSITY IN RAMADHAN

عن عبد الله بن عباس رضي الله عنهما، قال: "كان رسول الله صلى الله عليه

[26] Ibn Ḥibbān.

[27] Bukhārī.

وسلم أجود الناس، وكان أجود ما يكون في رمضان حين يلقاه جبريل، وكان
يلقاه في كل ليلة من رمضان، فيدارسه القرآن، فلرسول الله صلى الله عليه
وسلم أجود بالخير من الريح المرسلة"، رواه البخاري ـ

Ibn Abbās ﷺ says: "Rasūlullāh ﷺ was the most generous of all people, and he was even more generous in the month of Ramadhān when Jibra'īl ﷺ would come to visit him. Jibra'īl ﷺ used to visit him every night of Ramadhān and revise the Qur'ān with him. Indeed, Rasūlullāh ﷺ would be more generous with wealth than the wind that is blowing. [28]

Note: This means that just as heavy wind blows everything away, he would also give everything away. We normally spend more freely when we are happy. Rasūlullāh ﷺ would be extremely happy upon the regular visits of Jibra'īl ﷺ so he would spend everything he had or he would receive from somewhere.

[29] SADAQAH OF RAMADHAN IS THE MOST VIRTUOUS ONE

عن أنس رضي الله عنه : سئل النبي صلى الله عليه وسلم أي الصوم أفضل بعد
رمضان؟ قال شعبان لتعظيم رمضان قال: فأي الصدقة أفضل؟ قال "صدقة في
رمضان" رواه المنذري ـ

Anas ﷺ said: Rasūlullāh ﷺ was once asked, which fast is most virtuous after the fast of Ramadhan? He said the fast of Sha'bān in respect of Ramadhan." He ﷺ was asked: "Which Sadaqah is the most virtuous one? He replied: "Sadaqah during the month of Ramadhān." [29]

---

[28] Bukhārī.

[29] Munziri.

Note: Thawāb increases in Ramadhān therefore we should also increase our spending in the path of Allāh ﷻ.

[30] A SAAIM SHOULD KEEP HIS TONGUE UNDER CONTROL

عن أبي هريرة رضي الله عنه قال: إذا أصبح أحدكم يوما صائما فلا يرفث

ولا يجهل، فإن امرؤ شاتمه أو قاتله فليقل: إني صائم، إني صائم مسلم -

Abū Hurairah ﷺ narrates that Rasūlullāh ﷺ said, "When one of you is fasting, then he should not use obscene language, nor should he be foolish/irresponsible. And if someone swears at him or fights with him, he should say, "I am fasting." [30]

Note: Either he should say to the other person and turn away, or say it in the mind, i.e. remind himself of his duty towards the fast.

[31] ONE SHOULD NOT LIE TO ANYONE DURING THE FAST

عن أبي هريرة رضي الله عنه قال قال رسول الله صلى الله عليه وسلم من لم يدع

قول الزور والعمل به فليس لله حاجة في أن يدع طعامه وشرابه

رواه البخاري -

[30] Muslim.

Abū Hurairah رضي الله عنه narrates that Rasūlullāh ﷺ said: "Whoever does not abandon telling lies and acting upon lies, then Allāh is not in need of his abstaining from food and drink." [31]

Fasting is not just of the stomach, it is also of the other limbs. The fasting of the eyes, ears, tongue and even the heart and mind. So if a person continues with his bad habits during Sawm, it means that his Sawm is ineffective.

[32] REWARD OF SIYAAM AND QIYAM IS WIPED OUT DUE TO NOT CONTROLLING THE TONGUE

عَنْ أَبِيْ هُرَيْرَةَ عَنِ النَّبِيِّ صَلَّى اللهُ عَلَيْهِ وَسَلَّمَ ، قَالَ : " رُبَّ صَائِمٍ لَيْسَ لَهُ مِنْ صِيَامِهِ إِلا الْجُوْعُ وَرُبَّ قَائِمٍ لَيْسَ لَهُ مِنْ قِيَامِهِ إِلا السَّهَرُ رواه ابن ماجة -

Abū Hurairah رضي الله عنه narrates that Rasūlullāh ﷺ said, "Many people fast but gain nothing from their fast except hunger and thirst. And many people stand (Qiyām-ul-Layl) but they gain nothing but sleeplessness. [32]

This is what Sayyidunā Umar رضي الله عنه tried to explain in the following words: "The true fast is not to merely abstain from food and drink, rather a true fast is to abstain from futile activities and obscene talk." [33]

[33] BACKBITING WHILE FASTING REDUCES REWARD AND INCREASES THE EFFECTS OF HUNGER AND THIRST

[31] Bukhārī.

[32] Ibn Mājah.

[33] Ibn Abī Shaybah.

عَنْ عُبَيْدٍ مَوْلَى رَسُوْلِ اللهِ صَلَى اللهُ عَلَيْهِ وَسَلَّمَ ، أَنَّ امْرَأَتَيْنِ صَامَتَا عَلَى عَهْدِ رَسُوْلِ اللهِ صَلَّى اللهُ عَلَيْهِ وَسَلَّمَ ، فَقَالُوْا : يَا رَسُوْلَ اللهِ ، إِنَّ هَاهُنَا امْرَأَتَيْنِ صَامَتَا ، وَقَدْ كَادَتَا أَنْ تَمُوْتَا ؟ فَقَالَ النَّبِيُّ صَلَّى اللهُ عَلَيْهِ وَسَلَّمَ : "ائْتُوْنِيْ بِهِمَا"،فَجَاءَتَا ، فَدَعَا بِعُسٍّ أَوْ قَدَحٍ ، فَقَالَ لِإِحْدَاهُمَا : " قِي " ، فَقَاءَتْ مِنْ قَيْحٍ وَدَمٍ وَصَدِيْدٍ ، حَتَّى قَاءَتْ نِصْفَ الْقَدَحِ ، وَقَالَ لِلأُخْرَى : " قِي " ، فَقَاءَتْ مِنْ دَمٍ وَقِيْحٍ وَصَدِيْدٍ حَتَّى مَلأَتِ ا لْقَدَحَ ، فَقَالَ النَّبِيُّ صَلَّى اللهُ عَلَيْهِ وَسَلَّمَ : " إِنَّ هَاتَيْنِ صَامَتَا عَمَّا أَحَلَّ اللهُ لَهُمَا ، وَأَفْطَرَتَا عَلَى مَا حَرَّمَ اللهُ عَلَيْهِمَا ، جَلَسَتْ إِحْدَاهُمَا إِلَى الأُخْرَى فَجَعَلَتَا تَأْكُلانِ لُحُوْمَ النَّاسِ " رواه احمد

Ubaid ﵁, the freed slave of Rasūlullāh ﷺ, says "During the time of Rasūlullāh ﷺ, two women observed a fast for Ramadhān. A man came to Rasūlullāh ﷺ and said "Yā Rasūlullāh! There are two women who have observed fast, but they are very close to death. (Due to hunger, can they break their fast by eating something?) Rasūlullāh ﷺ said: "Go and bring them here." The two women came. Rasūlullāh ﷺ asked for a bowl, which was brought forth. He said to one of the women, "Vomit in this utensil." The woman vomited, blood and flesh came out of her mouth until she filled half the utensil. Then he said to the other woman, "Vomit in here." She did the same and she also vomited blood and flesh. Then Rasūlullāh ﷺ said, "These two women fasted from what Allāh has made halal for them however, they broke their fast with what Allāh has made harām upon them, they sat with one another, and kept consuming the flesh of people. [34]

[34] Ahmed.

Note: Where did the flesh come from when their stomachs were empty? They were dying of hunger? Allāh showed people a miracle that backbiting, in reality, is like eating the flesh of the other person.

[34] A SAAIM IS ALLOWED TO KISS HIS WIFE, PROVIDED HE CONTROLS HIMSELF

عن عائشة رضي الله عنها قالت: كان رسول الله صلى الله عليه وسلم يقبِّل وهو صائم، ويباشر وهو صائم، ولكنه أملكُكُم لأَرَبه. أخرجه البخاري ـ

Ā'ishā ﵂ says: "Rasūlullāh ﷺ used to kiss, hug and embrace (his wives) while fasting, and he had more control of his desires than any of you." [35]

[35] EATING BY MISTAKE, WHILE FORGETTING THE FAST, DOES NOT BREAK IT

عن أبي هريرة رضي الله عنه قال: قال رسول الله صلى الله عليه وسلم: من نسي وهو صائم فأكل أو شرب فليتمَّ صومه؛ فإنما أطعمه الله وسقاه أخرجه البخاري ـ

Abū Hurairah ﵁ narrates that Rasūlullāh ﷺ said: "When a fasting person forgets and eats and drinks, then he should complete his fast, because Allāh has fed him and Allāh has given him drink." [36]

---

[35] Bukhārī.

[36] Bukhārī.

[36] VOMIT ITSELF DOES NOT BREAK FAST, UNLESS IT'S ATTEMPTED AND DELIBERATE

عن أبي هريرة رضي الله عنه أن النبي صلى الله عليه وسلم قال:

من ذَرَعه القيء فليس عليه قضاء، ومن استقاء عمدًا فليقضِ أخرجه أحمد وأبو داود.

Abū Hurairah ﷺ narrates that Rasūlullāh ﷺ said, "Whoever is over-powered by vomit, there is no qadhā upon him (i.e. the fast is still valid). However, if one induces vomit, then upon him is qadhā." [37]

[37] BEING CAREFUL IN SAWM WHEN GARGLING AND CLEANING THE NOSE

عن لقيط بن صبرة رضي الله عنه قال: قلت: يا رسول الله، أخبرني عن الوضوء، قال: أسبغ الوضوء، وخلِّل بين الأصابع، وبالغ في الاستنشاق إلا أن تكون صائما رواه أحمد.

Laqīt Ibn Sabira ﷺ says I asked Rasūlullāh ﷺ to tell me about Wudhū! He said: Do Wudhū thoroughly and do khilāl in between the fingers and strive hard in putting water up the nose (and flushing it), except when you are fasting. [38]

Note: Because of the risk of water going up the nose and down in the throat, which would then break the fast.

---

[37] Ahmed, Abū Dāwūd.

[38] Ahmed.

[38] FASTING DURING TRAVELLING IS PERMITTED

عن حمزة بن عمرو الأسلمي رضي الله عنه أنه قال: يا رسول الله، أجد بي قو ة على الصيام في السفر، فهل عليَّ جناح؟ فقال رسول الله صلى الله عليه وسلم: هي رخصة من الله، فمن أخذ بها فحسن، ومن أحبَّ أن يصوم فلا جناح عليه أخرجه البخاري ـ

Hamzā Al-Aslamī ﷺ narrates that he said: Yā Rasūlullāh! I have the energy to fast while travelling, Is there anything wrong in this? Rasūlullāh ﷺ said: It (to not fast during travelling) is a Rukhsat (dispensation) from Allāh. Whoever takes it, it is good and whosoever would like to fast, there is no harm.[39]

Note: Some people say it is harām to fast while travelling. Even if such people go for Ụmrah to Makkāh Mukarramah, during Ramadhān, they don't fast. This Hadīth proves them wrong. They should fast, especially in this day and age where travelling is much easier in comparison to the previous eras.

[39] WHILE TRAVELLING, A SAAIM TRAVELLER SHOULD NOT LOOK DOWN ON A NON-SAAIM TRAVELLER

عن أبي سعيد الخدري وجابر بن عبد الله رضي الله عنهم قالا: سافرنا مع رسول الله صلى الله عليه وسلم فيصوم الصائم، ويفطر المفطر، فلا يعيب بعضهم على بعض. أخرجه مسلم ـ

---

[39] Bukhārī.

Abū Saeed ﷺ and Jābir ﷺ relate that we were traveling with Rasūlullāh ﷺ. While we were on the journey, some observed the fast, and others didn't. They did not blame each other, i.e. the ones who fasted didn't look down on those who didn't. And those who didn't, didn't blame those who did fast." [40]

[40] BREAKING A FAST OF RAMADHĀN FOR NO REASON, CANNOT BE ATONED FOR

عَنْ أَبِيْ هُرَيْرَةَ قَالَ : قَالَ رَسُوْلُ اللهِ صَلَّى اللهُ عَلَيْهِ وَسَلَّمَ مَنْ أَفْطَرَ يَوْمًا مِنْ رَمَضَانَ مِنْ غَيْرِ عُذْرٍ وَلَا مَرَضٍ لَمْ يَقْضِهِ صِيَامُ الدَّهْرِ وإِنْ صَامَهُ . رواه المنذري والبخاري في العلل وقال إبن بطال : ضعيف ـ

"Whoever breaks/fails to observe one day of the fast of Ramadhān, without a valid excuse, or any illness, fasting throughout their whole life wouldn't be enough to compensate for it, even if he were to do so. [41]

Note: This means he won't be able to recover the Thawāb of that single fast in any way. He does have to make qadhā if he missed it or even pay Kaffārah if he deliberately broke it.

[41] WHERE POSSIBLE, FAST SHOULD BE OPENED WITH A DATE

عن سليمان بن عامر عن النبي صلى الله عليه وسلم أنه قال: إذا أفطر أحدكم، فليفطر على تمر فإنه بركة، فإن لم يجد تمرًا، فالماء فإنه طهور رواه الترمذي،

[40] Muslim.

[41] Bukhārī.

Sulaimān bin Āamir ﷺ narrates that Rasūlullāh ﷺ said: "When one of you intends to break his fast, he should open it with a date because a date is full of blessings, if he cannot find a date, he should open his fast with water, because water is cleansing (purifying)." [42]

This means opening at sunset, when the fast has completed.

[42] DUĀ FOR IFTAAR

دعاء الإفطار :

عن معاذ بن زهرة قال : إن النبي صلى الله عليه وسلم كان إذا أفطر قال :

" اللهم لك صمت وعلى رزقك أفطرت " رواه أبو داود مرسلا ـ

Muāz Ibn Zahra ﷺ reports that when Rasūlullāh ﷺ broke his fast, he would say: "O Allāh! For you did I fast and with your given sustenance do I break it." [43]

كَانَ رَسُوْلُ اللهِ صَلَّى اللهُ عَلَيْهِ وَسَلَّمَ إِذَا أَ فطَرَ قَالَ ذَهَبَ الظَّمَأُ

وَابْتَلَّتِ الْعُرُوْقُ وَثَبَتَ الْأَجْرُ إِنْ شَاءَ اللهُ رواه ابو داود ـ

Another narration mentions that he would say: "The thirst is quenched, the veins are replenished, and hopefully the reward is set, by the will of Allāh." [44]

---

[42] Tirmīdhī.

[43] Abū Dāwūd, Mursal.

[44] Abū Dāwūd.

[43] STAYING AWAKE AT NIGHT DURING THE LAST ASHARAH

عن عائشة رضي الله عنها قالت: كان النبي صلى الله عليه وسلم إذا دخل
العشر شدَّ مئزره وأحيا ليله، وأيقظ أهله. أخرجه البخاري ومسلم ـ

Ā'ishā ﵂ reports: "When the last ten days of Ramadhān would begin, Rasūlullāh ﷺ would tighten his garment, and stay awake at night and awaken his family." [45]

Tightening the garment could mean staying away from his wives to keep busy in Ibādah. It could be a phrase used to say he would get ready to work hard.

[44] PERFORMING I'TIKĀF IN THE LAST ASHARAH

عَنْ عَائِشَةَ رضي الله عنها كان رسول الله صلى الله عليه وسلم
يعتكف العشر الأواخر من رمضان اخرجه البخاري ـ

Ā'ishā ﵂ reports: Rasūlullāh ﷺ would perform I'tikāf in the last ten days of Ramadhān. [46]

[45] Bukhārī, Muslim.

[46] Bukhārī.

[45] EXTRA EFFORT IN THE LAST 10 DAYS OF RAMADHĀN

عن عائشة رضي الله عنها قالت: كان رسول الله صلى الله عليه وسلم يجتهد في العشر الأواخر ما لا يجتهد في غيره أخرجه مسلم ـ

Ā'ishā ﵂ reports: Rasūlullāh ﷺ would strive [to do acts of worship] during the last ten days of Ramadhān more than he would in any other time. [47]

[46] SEARCHING FOR LAYLATUL QADR

عن عائشة رضي الله عنها أن رسول الله صلى الله عليه وسلم قال: تحروا ليلة القدر في الوتر من العشر الأواخر من رمضان أخرجه البخاري ـ

Ā'ishā ﵂ narrates that Rasūlullāh ﷺ said: "Search for Laylatul Qadr in the odd nights from the last 10 nights of Ramadhān." [48]

[47] GRAVE WARNING FOR NEGLECTING THE MONTH OF RAMADHĀN

حَدَّثَنِي سَعْدُ بْنُ إِسْحَاقَ بْنِ كَعْبِ بْنِ عُجْرَةَ، عَنْ أَبِيهِ، عَنْ كَعْبِ بْنِ عُجْرَةَ، قَالَ: قَالَ رَسُولُ اللهِ صَلَّى اللهُ عَلَيْهِ وَسَلَّمَ: " احْضُرُوا الْمِنْبَرَ " فَحَضَرْنَا، فَلَمَّا ارْتَقَى دَرَجَةً قَالَ: " آمِينَ "، فَلَمَّا ارْتَقَى الدَّرَجَةَ الثَّانِيَةَ قَالَ: " آمِينَ "، فَلَمَّا

[47] Muslim.

[48] Bukhārī.

ارْتَقَى الدَّرَجَةَ الثَّالِثَةَ قَالَ: " آمِينَ "، فَلَمَّا فَرَغَ نَزَلَ مِنَ الْمِنْبَرِ قَالَ: فَقُلْنَا له يا رَسُولَ الله لَقَدْ سَمِعْنَا الْيَوْمَ مِنْكَ شَيْئًا لَمْ نَكُنْ نَسْمَعُهُ قَالَ: " إِنَّ جِبْرِيلَ عَلَيْهِ السَّلَامِ عَرَضَ لِي فَقَالَ: بَعُدَ مَنْ أَدْرَكَ رَمَضَانَ فَلَمْ يُغْفَرْ لَهُ فَقُلْتُ: آمِينَ فَلَمَّا رَقِيتُ الثَّانِيَةَ قَالَ: بَعُدَ مَنْ ذُكِرْتَ عِنْدَهُ فَلَمْ يُصَلِّ عَلَيْكَ فَقُلْتُ: آمِينَ، فَلَمَّا رَقِيتُ الثَّالِثَةَ قَالَ: بَعُدَ مَنْ أَدْرَكَ وَالِدَيْهِ الْكِبَرَ عِنْدَهُ أَوْ أَحَدُهُمَا، فَلَمْ يُدْخِلَاهُ الْجَنَّةَ - أَظُنُّهُ قَالَ - فَقُلْتُ: آمِينَ "

Kạ'b Ibn Ujrah ﷺ says: Once Rasūlullāh ﷺ said: "Come close to the mimbar." We did accordingly. He ﷺ ascended the pulpit and said "Āmīn" on the first step, then again " Āmīn" on the second step and then " Āmīn" on the third step. When he descended, we asked him, "We heard something from you which we don't normally hear." He ﷺ said: Jibra'īl ﷺ appeared before me, and said, "May that person be distanced who despite obtaining the month of Ramadhān, was still not forgiven." I said, "Āmīn." When I ascended the second step he said, "May that person be distanced in whose presence you are mentioned but he does not confer blessings upon you." I said, " Āmīn." When I ascended the third step, he said, "Woe unto that person whose parents reach old age in his presence, yet he does not obtain Jannah (by serving them). I said, " Āmīn." [49]

Note: This means that those three are great blessings of Allāh ﷻ. Ramadhān, Rasūlullāh ﷺ and elderly parents. When someone violates their rights, they invite the curse of Allāh ﷻ. May Allāh ﷻ protect us. Āmīn.

[49] Baihaqī.

[48] KEEPING 6 NAFL FASTS OF SHAWWĀL

عن أبي أيوب الأنصاري رضي الله عنه أن رسول الله صلى الله عليه وسلم قال:

من صام رمضان ثم أتبعه ستًا من شوال، كان كصيام الدهر رواه مسلم -

Abū Ayyūb Al-Anṣārī ﷺ narrates that Rasūlullāh ﷺ said: "Whosoever fasts in Ramadhān, then follows it up by six fast of Shawwāl, it is as though he has kept fasts throughout the whole year. [50]

Note: This is because the reward of one deed is multiplied ten times, so 36 will be like 360. It is desirable (Mustahabb) to keep the six fasts of Shawwāl. The six fasts do not have to be kept consecutively. Ladies cannot combine the six of Shawwāl with their Qadhā of Ramadhān. They both have to be kept separately. It's like 4 Sunnah's of Zuhr and 4 Fardh. One cannot combine them both. The six fasts do not have to be kept consecutively.

MASĀʿIL OF FASTING

These are a few Masā'il regarding fasting. May Allāh ﷻ make them beneficial! Āmīn. I have gone over them with three doctors: Doctor Mazharuddin Sahib, Doctor Salīm and Doctor Liaqat. I also had them checked by our respected Muftī Shabbīr Sahib (Dāmat Barakātuhum).

DEFINITION

Sawm literally means 'to restrain oneself'. In Sharī'ah terminology, it means to refrain from these things throughout the day, eating, drinking and deriving sexual pleasure. Fasting is a great form of worship. One Hadīth says: "Everything has a door and the door of worship is fasting." It elevates a person from the animalistic nature to angelic ones.

[50] Muslim.

WHERE THE SUN DOES NOT SET OR RISE

There are countries in the world where the sun does not set for six months and it doesn't rise for the other six months. The Fuqahā say that the people of these countries should fast according to the timings of countries close to them. [51]

LONG HOURS

During the summer months, we have very long fasts. We should think of the short winter fasts we used to keep. When Allāh ﷻ made it easy for us during winter, then if Allāh ﷻ tests us a little bit in summer, we should accept Allāh's ﷻ order wholeheartedly. Some people find loopholes to avoid fasting. That should not be the case.

Some people claim to be diabetic and eat and drink freely in front of others who are fasting. If the person is elderly and a heavy diabetic, it could be understood. But many are healthy, go to work, or roam around the streets all day, smoke in the streets during Ramadhān etc. Such people should check their Imān.

UPON WHOM IS FASTING COMPULSORY ?

There are only three conditions for fasting to be Fardh:

[1] Islam
[2] Sanity
[3] Bulūgh (i.e. being mature)

When a person is Muslim, sane and mature, he/she has to fast. The only other condition is that he/she should not be a mā'zūr (a person who has a genuine excuse such as severe illness where there is no possibility of recovering).

---

[51] قلت: وكذلك يقدر لجميع الآجال كالصوم والزكاة (شامي)

WHEN DOES FASTING HAVE TO BE POSTPONED FOR A LATER DATE ?

[1] Haidh
[2] Nifaas

A woman on her period or post-natal bleeding is not permitted to fast. She has to postpone fasting for other days.

GENUINE EXCUSES FOR NOT FASTING OR POSTPONING

[1] Being sick
[2] A traveller
[3] Pregnant
[4] Breastfeeding
[5] Extreme weakness which can lead to illness
[6] Insanity
[7] Being unconscious for long periods, as in coma
[8] Being in the battlefield, striving for the cause of Allāh ﷻ

Sick people and women who are pregnant or breastfeeding are obliged to fast. However, illness can excuse a person from fasting if one reasonably fears that the act of fasting would increase the sickness or slow the recovery process. The same ruling applies to a woman who is pregnant or breastfeeding and reasonably fears that fasting will harm her or her baby. Reasonable fear is known by:

[1] Manifest signs.
[2] A relevant past experience.
[3] The notification of an upright, Muslim doctor/expert. [52]

[52] Shurunbulali, Maraqi al-Falah; Shurunbulali, Imdad al-Fattah

A traveller is also excused from fasting if he initiates his journey before the time of Fajr enters. However, it is better that he fasts providing that this does not cause undue hardship. If a person begins fasting a day of Ramadhān and then travels, he is obliged to complete his fast.

When these excuses finish, one has to fast. If illness continues and the person is unable to make Qadhā at a later date, then they have to give fidyā, which is the amount of Sadaqatul Fitr for every missed fast.

NIYYAH

Intention is in the heart. It does not have to be said verbally. Eating Suhoor is an indication of the intent. However, if one does want to make a verbal intention, there is no reason to stop them. One could say:

وبصوم غد نويت من شهر رمضان ـ

"I intend to fast tomorrow for Ramadhān."

If one stays hungry and thirsty, without intending to fast, the fast will not be counted.

Note:

[1] One should try to keep all fasts properly. If one breaks a fast or does not keep it at all, it is impossible to gain the reward, which could equal that of the missed fast. One Hadīth says:

من أفطر يوما من رمضان من غير رخصة ولا
مرض لم يقض عنه صوم الدهر كله وان صامه [53]

"Whoever misses (or breaks) a fast of Ramadhān without a genuine reason, or any sickness, fasting for the whole life cannot make up for it, even if he were to do so." [54]

---

[53] رواه المنذرى عن ابى هريرة مرفوعا

[54] Munziri.

[2] One needs to keep a golden rule in mind:

الفطر مما دخل وليس مما خرج [55]

"A fast breaks by what goes in the body, not by what comes out."

Therefore, if one has a blood test, or a diabetic person checks his sugar level, or someone has cupping done (Hijāmah) etc, his fast will not be broken. It will be broken by something which enters the cavity of the body, i.e. which goes either down the throat into the stomach or into the brain. This can be through the throat, nose, ears, anus or the private parts.

However, there are two exceptions:

[1] القيء vomiting: If one intentionally and deliberately draws vomit from the stomach (by sticking a finger down his throat, applying pressure to his stomach or deliberately smelling a repulsive odour) and it is a mouthful, the fast will be broken – there is a consensus upon this. If the vomit was less than a mouthful, then Imām Muhammad's ﷺ research is that it will still be broken. However, Imām Abū Yūsuf ﷺ says it will NOT be broken. Ihtiyaat (caution) will be to take Imām Muhammad's ﷺ opinion. Allāmah Aynī ﷺ writes:

" الأصل فى العبادات الاحتياط " [56]

وان إستقاء أى طلب القيء عامدا اى متذكرا لصومه ان كان ملأ الفم فسد بالإجماع مطلقا. وإن أقلّ لا عند الثانى وهو الصحيح لكن ظاهر الرواية كقول محمد انه يفسد كما فى الفتح عن الكافى. [57]

---

[55] رواه البخارى عن ابن عباس ورواه البيهقى مرفوعا ورواه ابو يعلى الموصلى عن عائشة مرفوعا

[56] البناية ص 1400/ 2

[57] شامى ص 393 / 3 تحفة ص 68

وعن ابى هريرة رضى الله عنه قال قال رسول الله من ذرعه القئ

وهو صائم فليس عليه قضاء وان استقاء عمدا فليقض [58]

If the vomiting was UNINTENTIONAL and without the person's own doing, it does NOT break the fast, even if it was a mouthful.

If part of the vomit goes back down the throat, then if it went back down on its own, the fast is not broken. However, if it was deliberately swallowed, the fast is broken.

اذا قاء او استقاء ملء الفم او دونه وعاد بنفسه او اعاد

او اخرج فلا فطر على الاصح الا فى الاعادة [59]

[2] المنى Semen: If semen comes out of the body due to sexual intercourse or masturbation, or any other deliberate activity, the fast will be broken, similarly, if there was no intercourse, just foreplay of hugging and kissing, which resulted in semen coming out, the fast will break.

...أَوْ قَبَّلَ وَلَوْ قُبْلَةً فَاحِشَةً بِأَنْ يُدَغْدِغُ أَوْ يَمُصُّ شَفَتَيْهَا (أَوْ لَمَسَ) وَلَوْ بِحَائِلٍ لَا يَمْنَعُ الْحَرَارَةَ...(فَأَنْزَلَ).. قَضى فِى الصُّوَرِ كُلِّهَا [60]

However, if one forgot he was fasting and had sexual intercourse, or had a wet dream and semen came out, or semen was released just by looking, or thinking and without any physical action, the fast will NOT break.

[58] رواه الترمذى وابو داود. احكا رمضان ص 287

[59] هندية ص 204 / 1 تحفة ص 66

[60] شامى ص 379 / 3 فتاوى دار العلوم ص 417 / 6 تحفة ص 70

منها لو أكل الصائم او شرب او جامع ناسيا لصومه [61]

او احتلم..الخ لم يفطر [62]

Note: المنى or semen is that thick sticky substance which is released upon ejaculation, followed by loosening of the organ. There is another substance called المذى Mazī. This is some discharge which is released during foreplay or upon thinking of the act. There is no ejaculation involved. This sticky discharge does not break the fast.

اِذا مص الصائم امرأته وأمذى لا يفسد صومه [63]

وكذا إذا نظر إلى امرأة فأمنى لما بينا فصار كالمتفكر اذا أمنى [64][65]

Note: لواطة . If two homosexuals perform the act of intercourse, their fast will be broken. Both will have to keep Qadhā and give Kaffārah.

ثم عندنا كما تجب الكفارة بالوقاع على الرجل تجب على المرأة ـ

قوله "تجب على المرأة" قال على المفعول به كان افيه. [66]

Note: Homosexual acts are harām and a major sin in the eyes of Allāh ﷻ.

We now put forward an anatomy of the body to explain what breaks the fast and what doesn't.

---

[61] مراقى الفلاح ص 360 تحفة ص 62

[62] شامى 367 / 3 تحفة ص 63

[63] تاتارخانية ص 371 / 2 أحسن الفتاوى ص 441 / 4

[64] الهداية مع فتح القدير ص 333 / 2

[65] احكام ص 391

[66] الهداية و فتح القدير ص 342 / 2

MOUTH

If someone went to the dentist for cleaning, for a filling, or for extracting a tooth, his or her fast is at a huge risk. There is the possibility that some liquid or blood could go down the throat. It is nearly impossible to avoid it so the fast will be broken. If bleeding from the gums occurs both spontaneously or as a result of treatment, and the blood went down the throat, the fast will be broken (though it wouldn't break if one spat it out) and nothing went down the throat.

Swallowing capsules or pain killer tablets will break the fast. However, if the medicine was in liquid form and just a drop was placed on the tongue, it dissolved on the tongue and did not go down the throat, it will not break the fast.[67] This can be the case with some homeopathic medicines, or an angina tablet which is placed under the tongue. [68]

Swallowing saliva mixed with blood, where the blood is more than the saliva, will break the fast. Likewise, swallowing another person's saliva (such as the wife's after kissing), or one's own saliva after taking it out in the hand and then licking it, will break the fast (not if it was still in the mouth). If something edible was stuck between the teeth, one should spit it out. However, if one swallowed it without taking it out of the mouth, and it was smaller than a chickpea, the fast will not break. If it was larger, or smaller but one took it out in the hand and then put it back in the mouth to swallow it, the fast will break.

وَإِنْ أَكَلَ مَا بَيْنَ أَسْنَانِهِ لَمْ يُفْسِدْ إِنْ كَانَ قَلِيلًا وَإِنْ كَانَ كَثِيرًا يُفْسِدُ، وَالْحِمَّصَةُ وَمَا فَوْقَهَا كَثِيرٌ، وَمَا دُونَهَا قَلِيلٌ، وَإِنْ أَخْرَجَهُ وَأَخَذَهُ بِيَدِهِ ثُمَّ أَكَلَ يَنْبَغِي أَنْ يُفْسِدَ[69]

---

[67] أحكام ص 227

[68] الفتاوى اللُّجْنَة

[69] الفتاوى الهندية ص 252 / 1 تحفة ص 64

If there was some wetness left in the mouth after gargling and throwing the water out, and it went down the throat with the saliva, it will not break the fast.

ولو بقى بلل بعد مضمضة فابتلعه مع البزاق لم يفطر [70]

Swallowing a stone, mud, metal or anything that is not edible will break the fast. However, if a fly or a mosquito went down the throat whilst yawning, the fast will not break. Similarly, if particles of Miswaak remained in the mouth and went down despite the effort to spit it out, the fast will not break.

The fast will break by water going down the throat whilst gargling, even by mistake. This is important to remember whilst doing Wudhū or Ghusl. Gargle lightly. One Hadīth says:

وبالغ فى المضمضة الا ان تكون صائما [71]

However, according to Imām Shāfi'ee's ﷺ research, the fast will not break by such mistakes.

If someone was forced to eat or drink, by an enemy or due to fear of life, or he fell ill whilst fasting and the doctors administered some medicine, the fast will be broken, though only Qadhā will be necessary, not Kaffārah. Chewing gum, Paan (betel leaves), tobacco, Niswaar etc. will also break the fast. [72]

If someone was chewing Paan, fell asleep with the Paan in his mouth, and woke up after Subhe Sadiq, his fast will not be counted. If someone gargled after having Paan but some reddish colour was left and went down the throat with the saliva, it will not break the fast.

وان أفطر خطأ كان تمضمض فسبقه الماء او شرب نائما قضى فقط [73]

---

[70] هندية ص 203 / 1 تحفة ص 65

[71] ذكره ابن العربى فى عارضة الاحوذى ص 189 / 2

[72] احكام ص 258

[73] شامى زكريا ص 373 / 2 تحفة ص 68

Blood from a nose bleed which goes down the throat will break the fast.

اذا دخل رُفَاعُهُ حلقه فسد صومه [74]

SMOKING CIGARETTES

Smoking cigarettes or cigars breaks the fast. With regards to Kaffārah along with Qadhā, there are two opinions of the Muftiyāne Kirām.

[1] Muftī Salmān Mansūrpūrī is of the opinion that only Qadhā is necessary, not Kaffārah. He writes:

وبه علم حكم شرب الدخان ونظمه الشرنبلالى فى شرحه
على الوهبانية بقوله "وشاربه فى الصوم لا شكّ يفطر" [75]

[2] However, Muftī Radhāul Haq Sahib of Dārul Uloom Zakarīyā writes that Kaffārah will also be Wājib. This is the opinion of our Muftī Shabbīr Sahib and Muftī Sūfī Tāhir Sahib.

مفتی رضاء الحق کہتے ہیں عام طور سے سیگریٹ پینے والے سیگریٹ کو نفع بخش سمجھتے ہیں
لہٰذا قضاء و کفارہ دونوں لازم ہیں۔ اور پاس بیٹھنے والا حلق میں دھواں کھینچ کر داخل کرے [76]
تو (اسکا بھی) روزہ فاسد ہو جایگا اور قضاء واجب ہو گی۔

Muftī Radhāul Haq says, "Usually those who smoke cigarettes do so because they know it benefits them, thus Qadhā and Kaffārah will both become

[74] تاتارخانية ص 369 / 2 تحفة ص 68

[75] شامى زكريا ص 366 / 3 فتاوى دار العاوم ص 365 / 6 تحفة ص 69

[76] Passive Smoking.

necessary. Also, if someone who was sitting next to a smoker intentionally draws in the smoke, his fast will also break and Qadhā will be necessary."

قال الشرنبلالى ويلزمه التكفير لو ظن نافعا وكذا قال الطحطاوى حاشيته على المراقى ص 665

وعلى هذا البدعة التى ظهرت الآن وهو الدخان إذا شربه فى لزوم الكفارة ...فمن قال اذا التغذى ما يميل اليه الطبع وتنقض به شهوة البطن ألزم به الكفارة. انتهى

SMOKING HUQQA OR SHISHA

Smoking Huqqa or Shisha, will also break the fast, Qadhā will be necessary and in some cases Kaffārah also becomes necessary. This is when something beneficial is added to it e.g. fruit flavourings etc.

حقہ سے روزہ ٹوٹجاتا ہے اور قضاء لازم ہوتی ہے بعض صورتوں میں کفارہ بھی لازم ہوتا ہے یعنی اسُے نفع بخش سمجھا تو کفارہ قضاء دونوں لازم ہونگے ورنہ صرف قضاء [77]

If smoke goes down the throat without any wrongdoing, the fast will not break e.g. while cooking in the kitchen.

او دخل حلقه غبار او ذباب او دخان ولو ذاكرا استحسانا [78]

---

[77] فتاوی دار العلوم دیوبند ص 6/419

[78] شامی زکریا 366 / 3 بیروت 367 / 3 تحفة ص 63

ASTHMA PUMP

If someone had an asthma attack and used the asthma pump, the fast will be broken according to the Hanafī research. This is because the pump contains medicine, which goes down the throat. [79] [80]

Some people say that it does not break the fast, because the medicine goes into the lungs, not down to the stomach. However, this is not true. The Fuqahā have said that smoking cigarettes breaks the fast, and that smoke also goes down to the lungs and not the stomach. Therefore, anything that is swallowed or inhaled deliberately should nullify the fast. Secondly, although most of it goes in the lungs, some of it does go down the throat and into the stomach.

One may ask, "What should such a person do?" The answer would be to try and avoid the pump as much as possible. Avoid heavy activities, which make one short of breath – take it easy during Ramadhān. If one can take time off during Ramadhān they should do so. Then, if it becomes necessary to take it, use it, but do Tashabbuh Bissaimeen i.e. emulate those who are fasting and keep Qadhā during the shorter days of winter.

If the person is elderly or unable to keep Qadhā, he/she could give Fidyā for the fasts.

LOCAL ANAESTHETIC

Local anaesthetic either applied to the skin or injected into the body will not break the fast. General anaesthetic gases given through the mouth and nose would break the fast if there is some other solution mixed in them, which normally is the case. [81]

---

[79] قارى عبد الباسط

[80] محمد. احكام رمضان المارك ص 228

[81] فتاوى اللُّجْنَة

USE OF OXYGEN

If someone needs oxygen and has to take it while moving around, this will not break the fast, because it is just air compressed in a bottle and taken to ease the breathing. There is no substance in it. [82]

USING PERFUME

If someone sprayed perfume on himself, he felt the taste of it in his throat, this will not break the fast. [83]

TASTING FOOD

To taste food or to chew it and then throw it out without anything going down the throat is Makrūh if there is no genuine reason (Udhr). If it was done due to a genuine reason, it will not be Makrūh. In both cases the fast will not break. A genuine reason could be an ill-tempered husband who could get very angry at the wife if the salt or masala was not proper. Chefs working in restaurants could also be excused if the boss is a hot-tempered person and the job could be at risk if mistakes are made. However, it would be better to have it tasted by a non-Muslim colleague. One should avoid putting the fast at risk. [84]

TEARS OR SWEAT

Tears or sweat going down the throat. If just a drop or two went down and no salty taste is felt in the throat, the fast will not break. However, if it was a lot, or a little but the taste was felt, it will break.

---

[82] جديد فقهى مسائل ص 128 أحكام ص 227

[83] أحكام 227

[84] أحكام ص 229

اذا دخل الدمع فى فم الصائم ان كان قليلا نحو القطرة او القطرتين لا يفسد صومه لان الإحتراز عنه غير ممكن. وان كان كثيرا حتى وجد ملوحته فى جميع فمه وابتلعه فسد صومه وكذا الجواب فى عرق الوجه [85]

GINGIVITIS

This is where the gums constantly bleed and sometimes blood goes down the throat, will this break the fast? If one spits the blood out, it will not affect the fast. However, if one swallows it and the blood was more than the saliva or equal to it, the fast will break. If blood was only minimal, the fast will not break, unless he felt the taste of the blood when he swallowed it.

لو خرج الدم من بين اسنانه ودخل حلقه يفسد لم يصل الى جوفه.

أما اذا وصل فان غلب الدم او تساويا فسد والا لا إلا اذا وجد طعمه [86]

EXTRACTING THE TOOTH WHILST FASTING

If one's tooth was loose and it came out or it was extracted smoothly without any bleeding, the fast will not break. However, if it involved bleeding and blood went down the throat, it will break the fast. Qadhā will be necessary.

قلت ومن هذا يُعلم من قلع ضرسه فى رمضان ودخل الدم الى جوفه فى النهار ولو نائما فيجب عليه القضاء [87]

BRUSHING THE TEETH WITH TOOTHPASTE

It is Makrūh to brush the teeth with toothpaste, or use mouthwash whilst fasting. This is because of the taste of the paste and because of the risk of

---

[85] شامى ص 178 / 3 أحكام

[86] شامى ص 367 / 3 احكام ص 234

[87] شامى ص 368 / 3 أحكام ص 233

something going down the throat. If something did go down the throat, it will break the fast as well. One should use a Miswaak. If the Miswaak was fresh and it had a pleasant taste that would not harm the fast. It will not even be Makrūh, nor will it affect the fast.

وكره له ذوق شئ ومضغه [88]

ولا بأس بالسواك الرطب واليابس فى الغداة والعشى ولا يكره الكحل

ولا دهن شاربه كذا فى الكنز [89]

WOMEN APPLYING LIPSTICK

If there is risk that the lipstick will go down the throat at some stage, it will be Makrūh to apply. If it does go down the throat, it will break the fast, otherwise it won't. [90]

NOSE

If one was cleaning the nose in Wudhū or Ghusl, and he pulled the water up his nose so hard that it went down the throat, his fast will be broken.

If one snuffed some medicine up his nose or sniffed some drugs or glue etc. his fast will be broken. Similarly, if one used Bukhoor and deliberately took smoke up his nose, his fast will be broken.

لو ادخل حلقه الدخان اى بأى صورة كان أفطر لامكان التحرز عنه [91]

---

[88] شامى بيروت ص 352 / 3 فتاوى دار العلوم ص 404 / 6 تحفة ص 74

[89] علمجيرى ص 199 / 1 جواهر الفقه ص 379 / 1 تحفة ص 26

[90] تحفة ص 74

[91] شامى ص 366 / 3 تحفة ص 67

If one had the flu and put some Vicks in a bucket of hot water and inhaled the steam into his nose by covering his head with a towel or something, his fast will be broken.

EARS

If one was to put some medicine, eardrops or oil inside his ears, the fast will break. This could be because the substance travels up to the brain and nullifies the fast. Only Qadhā will be necessary, not Kaffārah.

ومن احتقن او استعط او أقطر فى أذنه أفطر ولا كفارة عليه [92]

If someone cleaned the ears with cotton buds or pierced something in the ears and took some dirt out, the fast will not be broken. Even if one re-entered the piece with the dirt stuck to it, the fast will not break.

واذا حكّ اذنه بعود فأخرج العود وعلى رأسه شئ من الدّرن ثم أدخل
ثانيا مع ذلك الدرن ثم أخرجه وبقى الدرن فى الأذن لا يفسد [93]

If water went into the ears, it will be one of two scenarios:

[1] It went inside without any wrongdoing from the person. E.g. one jumped into a swimming pool or river, or one was having a shower and water went into the ear by mistake. This will not break the fast as there is no intent here and water is not something, which does good to the ears. Plus, it is normally unavoidable, so Sharī'ah will be flexible.

[2] However, if one deliberately thrusts water inside, or puts medicine or oil, then the Saheeh Qowl (correct opinion) is that the fast will break.

---

[92] هداية ص 220 / 1

[93] الفتاوى تاتارخانية ص 364 / 2 شامى ص 367 / 3 أحكام ص 251

صائم اغتسل فدخل الماء فى أذنه لا شئ عليه لانه لم يوجد الفطر صورة ولا معنى [94]

قال الشامى إن دخل لا يفسد وان أدخله يفسد فى الصحيح لانه وصل الى الجوف بفعله فلا يعتبر فيه صلاح البدن [95]

قال قاضيخان ولو خاض الماء فدخل الماء أذنه لا يفسد صومه. وان صب الماء فى أذنه اختلفوا فيه والصحيح الفساد لانه وصل الى الجوف بفعله فلا يعتبر فيه صلاح البدن [96]

EYES

If someone applied eye drops or artificial tears to the eyes, this will not invalidate the fast, as there is no direct passage from the eyes to the stomach or the brain.

قال الكاسانى انه ليس للعين منفذ الى الجوف [97]

If one applied Surmah (Kohl) to the eyes, the fast will not break, even if he felt the taste in his throat or the colour appeared in the saliva. This is because it is narrated in the Hadīth that Rasūlullāh ﷺ applied Surmah whilst he was fasting.

عَنْ عَائِشَةَ، قَالَتْ : اكْتَحَلَ رَسُوْلُ اللهِ صَلَّى اللهُ عَلَيْهِ وَسَلَّمَ وَهُوَ صَائِمٌ [98]

---

[94] الفتاوى الغياثية ص 53 أحكام ص 252

[95] شامى ص 367 / 3

[96] الفتاوى الخانية مع الهندية ص 209 / 1 احكام ص 254

[97] بدائع الصنائع ص 635 / 2

[98] ابن ماجه 1678

عَنْ أَنَسِ بْنِ مَالِكٍ قَالَ : جَاءَ رَجُلٌ إِلَى النَّبِيِّ صَلَّى اللهُ عَلَيْهِ وَسَلَّمَ فَقَالَ: اشْتَكَتْ عَيْنِي، أَفَأَكْتَحِلُ وَأَنَا صَائِمٌ ؟ قَالَ: نَعَمْ. [99]

قَالَ الكَاسَانِي وَلَا بَأْسَ أَنْ يَكْتَحِلَ الصَّائِمُ بِالْإِثْمِدِ وَغَيْرِهِ، وَلَوْ فَعَلَ لَا يُفْطِرُهُ وَإِنْ وَجَدَ طَعْمَهُ فِي حَلْقِهِ عِنْدَ عَامَّةِ الْعُلَمَاءِ لِمَا رَوَيْنَا «أَنَّ رَسُولَ اللهِ – صَلَّى اللهُ عَلَيْهِ وَسَلَّمَ – اكْتَحَلَ وَهُوَ صَائِمٌ» وَلِمَا ذَكَرْنَا أَنَّهُ لَيْسَ لِلْعَيْنِ مَنْفَذٌ إِلَى الْجَوْفِ [100]

PRIVATE PARTS

Sexual intercourse breaks the fast. Whether ejaculation takes place or not, is irrelevant. Both parties will have to keep Qadhā and give Kaffārah as well.

If someone masturbates whilst fasting, the fast will break. Qadhā will be Wājib, not Kaffārah. Kaffārah not being Fardh is because deriving sexual pleasure is only complete when two parties are involved, so the effect is also lessened when no one else is involved.

اذا عالج ذكره بيده حتى أمنى...عامة مشائخنا
استحسنو وأفتوا بالفساد. وفى الخلاصة: لا كفارة عليه [101]

The act in itself is Makrūh Taḥrīmī (prohibitively disliked) according to Hanafī research, as Allāmah ibn Humām ﷺ has stated in Fathul Qadeer. Imām Mālik ﷺ is of the opinion that it's Harām. Faqeeh Abul Layth Samarqandī ﷺ, who is a Hanafī, also classed it as Harām. [102]

The Daleel (proof) for both opinions is in the Ayah:

---

[99] ترمذی 726 . احکام ص 219

[100] بدائع ص 635 / 2

[101] تاتارخانية ص 0 / 2 الهندية ص 205 / 1 فتح القدير ونهاية ص 234 / 2 احكام ص 290

[102] تنبيه ص 358

وَالَّذِيْنَ هُمْ لِفُرُوْجِهِمْ حٰفِظُوْنَ ۝

اِلَّا عَلٰى اَزْوَاجِهِمْ اَوْ مَا مَلَكَتْ اَيْمَانُهُمْ فَاِنَّهُمْ غَيْرُ مَلُوْمِيْنَ ۝

فَمَنِ ابْتَغٰى وَرَآءَ ذٰلِكَ فَاُولٰٓئِكَ هُمُ الْعٰدُوْنَ ۝

"And who guard their private parts. Except from their wives or from those (bondwomen whom) they own, as they are not to be blamed. And whosoever seeks other than this, they are the ones who exceed the limits." [103]

Masturbation is exceeding the limits. There is also a Hadīth narrated here:

نَاكِحُ الْيَدِ مَلْعُوْنٌ [104]

"One who derives pleasure with his own hands is Mal'oon (cursed)."

However, this is not proven to be a Hadīth of Rasūlullāh ﷺ. It is most likely the saying of someone from the Salaf, which was quoted as a Hadīth.

قال جريج سألت عطاء عنه فقال مكروه سمعت

ان قوما يحشرون وأيديهم حُبالى فأظن أنهم هؤلآء [105]

Jurayj ﷺ says that he asked Ataa (ibn Abi Rabaah) ﷺ about it. He said, "It is disliked. I have heard that certain people will be resurrected on the Day of Judgement while their hands will be (swollen) like heavily pregnant (women). I think it is these people."

وعن سعيد ابن جبير قال عذب الله امة يعبثون بمذاكيرهم [106]

[103] Qur'ān 23:5-7.

[104] كشف الخفاء ص 291 / 2

[105] تنبيه الغافلين ص 358

[106] تنبيه الغافلين ص 359

Saeed Ibn Jubair ﷺ says, "Allāh punished a nation who used to play with their genitals."

What if a woman masturbates by inserting something in her vagina to derive sexual pleasure? I could not find this Mas'ala in Fiqhi books. The principles of Fiqh state that if the inserted item was dry and it did not fully disappear i.e. part of it remained out, the fast would not break. However, if the object fully disappeared, or it had some gel on it or it was taken out with some discharge on it and then re-entered, then the fast will break. Qadhā will be necessary.

ولو ادخل اصبعه فى استه او المرأة فى فرجها لا يفسد. وهو المختارالا اذا كانت مبتلّة بالماء او الدهن فحينئذ يفسد لوصول الماء او الدهن. هكذا فى الظهيرة [107]

"If someone inserted his finger in his anus, or a woman in her vagina, the fast will not break (according to the preferred opinion). However, if the finger was wet with water or oil, the fast will break, because the water and the oil reach inside."

Based on this, we can say her fast will break.

If a woman inserted some medicine into the vagina, the fast will break.

قال فى بحر الرائق "لأن الإقطار فى قبل المرأة يفسد الصوم بلا خلاف على الصحيح [108]

In Ahsan ul Fatāwā it is written that if some cream is applied to the outer layer of the vagina, due to a rash, the fast would not break. The other is the

---

[107] الفتاوى الهندية ص 204 / 1 احكام ص 295

[108] البحر الرائق ص 488 / 2 تحفة ص 71

inner part, which is round. If medicine is inserted there, or the cream reaches inside, the fast will break. [109]

If something was placed inside a woman's private part, it would break her fast. This is because in a woman's body, there is a natural passage which takes the substance inside, so her fast would be broken. [110]

VAGINAL EXAMINATION AND SMEAR TEST

A woman who attends for a smear test or vaginal examination whilst fasting. If the mechanical instrument used for the examination, or the hand (in the case of a manual examination) was dry, it would not break the fast. However, if there was some gel on it, or it was withdrawn and reinserted with some discharge on it, it will break the fast. [111] It would be safer not to have such tests during Ramadhān.

Some ladies ask if Ghusl becomes Fardh after a smear test. The answer is no. Ghusl only becomes Fardh upon sexual intercourse or the ejaculation of semen. Neither takes place here, so Ghusl will not become Fardh. However, Wudhū will break because of the discharge that comes out.

If a woman was raped during her fast (Allāh forbid!) or intercourse was forced upon her whilst she was sleeping or unconscious, her fast will break. She will only have to keep Qadhā. The other person will have to keep Qadhā and give Kaffārah as well.

وان كانت مكرهة فعليها القضاء دون الكفارة

وكذا اذا كانت مكرهة فى الإبتداء ثم طاوعته بعد ذلك [112]

If someone touched the body of another person, was aroused, and as a result ejaculated, the fast will break. Only Qadhā will be necessary. If ejaculation did not take place, the fast will not break. [113]

---

[109] Ahsan ul Fatāwā Pg.438/4. Masā'il Raf'at Qasimi Pg.114.

[110] Jadeed Fiqhi Masā'il Pg.97.

[111] تحفة ص 71

[112] عالمجيرى ص 205 / 1 تحفة ص 71

[113] مسائل ص 80

If one was sitting with his wife and ejaculated just by looking at her, (this happens due to weakness, medical attention should be sought), the fast will not break, as there was no touching involved. Similar will be the case of looking at a non-Mahram and releasing semen without touching, masturbation etc.

If a husband inserted his finger in the wife's vagina, his fast will not break. With regards to her fast, there is some detail. If the finger was wet at the time of inserting, or it was dry but he extracted it and then reinserted it, then the wife's fast will break. She will have to keep Qadhā, but Kaffārah will not be necessary. [114]

If a husband inserted his finger in the vagina of the wife to apply some medicine, then they were aroused by sexual desire, they thought their fast was broken so they had intercourse, their fast will be broken, and they will both have to keep Qadhā. As for the Kaffārah, the husband will have to give Kaffārah, not the wife. This is because her fast was already broken by the insertion of the medicine, and then the intercourse took place.

If two women were to derive sexual pleasure with one another, (which is Harām) and they reached a state of orgasm, their fast will be broken. They will have to keep Qadhā, but Kaffārah will not be Fardh upon them. If they did not reach the state of orgasm, the fast will not break. [115]

Note: It is not a condition for the validity of the fast that a person be free from the state of major ritual impurity (janāba). The mother of the believers, Ā'ishā (Allāh be pleased with her) said, "Fajr would enter during the month of Ramadhān and the Messenger of Allāh (Allāh bless him and give him peace) would be in a state of major ritual purity from other than a sexual dream (i.e. because of sexual relations). He would perform the purificatory bath and fast (that day)." [116]

Likewise, if one intended to fast during the night and woke up within Fajr time in a state of major ritual impurity, then one must perform the

[114] Ahsan ul Fatāwā 9447 Vol.4 / Masā'il Raf'at Pg.117.

[115] Hindiyyah Pg.20 Vol.2. Masā'il Pg.113.

[116] Muslim.

purificatory bath (ghusl) for the sake of the validity of one's prayers, fast this day, and the fast is considered valid.

INSERTING A CATHETER

If a man was having trouble passing water, and a catheter was inserted into the bladder, will his fast break? Imām Abū Hanīfā ﵀ and Imām Muhammad ﵀ are of the opinion that his fast will not break. This is because there is no direct passage [117] between the urethra and the stomach, therefore, the fast will not break. [118] However, if a woman was to insert some medicine in her vagina, her fast will break as there is a direct passage to her stomach. [119]

ANUS

If one uses Enema to empty the bowels, this will break the fast as it has a direct link to the digestive system.

واذا احتقن يفسد صومه [120]

If someone inserted a suppository into the anus or applied cream e.g. for piles, the fast will only break if the substance reached up to the place of 'Huqna' (up to the level of the rectum). This can only happen if the suppository is inserted with force and the effect can be felt inside, or the medicine travels slowly upwards. One should be careful and avoid it during the fast. Use it at night time if possible.

The same ruling will apply if a dry piece of cloth/tissue or something was inserted in such a way that it disappeared inside the body, the fast will break. If it did not totally disappear, part of it remained outside, the fast will not

---

[117] منفذ أصلى

[118] عالمجيرى ص 104 / 1.

[119] مشائل رفعة قاسمى ص 115 . جديد فقهى مسائل ص 97

[120] تاتارخانية ص 365 / 2 تحفة ص 71

break. Where the fast breaks, only Qadhā will be necessary. Kaffārah will not apply. [121]

If someone had intercourse into the anus of a man or a woman, both parties' fast will break and Qadhā and Kaffārah will both be necessary. [122]

ثم عندنا كما تجب الكفارة بالوقاع على الرجل تجب على المرأة -

قوله "تجب على المرأة" لو قال على المفعول به كان أفيد [123]

Note: the act itself is Harām. It has been declared Harām in the Tawrāt, Zaboor, Injeel and the Qur'ān; all four religious books. The gravity of the sin increases if it is committed during the month of Ramadhān. Such people should seize the initiative of Ramadhān to do Taubah and repent wholeheartedly.

THE REST OF THE BODY

If someone had an open wound in the abdomen or the brain, and applied medicine, which went inside, the fast will be broken and a Qadhā will have to be kept.

وما وصل الى الجوف او الى الدماغ من المخارق الأصلية فسد الصوم [124]

If someone had an operation during Ramadhān, if nothing reached inside the stomach or the brain, the fast will be ok. However, if general anaesthetic was administered, then the medicine goes inside. Therefore, the fast will break.

If someone went for dialysis during Ramadhān, then one has to remember that this only cleans the blood, flushes the kidneys and nothing reaches the stomach or the brain. Therefore, dialysis itself will not break the fast.

---

[121] Masā'il Raf'at Qasimi Pg.81.

[122] احكام ص 298

[123] الهداية و فتح القدير ص 342 / 2

[124] بدائع الصنائع ص 606 / 2

However, if one consumed some food or drink after dialysis, the fast will break.[125]

If the kidney patient struggles to fast on the day of dialysis, he could leave that day's fast and fast on the other days. Then, when Ramadhān finishes, he could make up for the days missed. If he was old and so ill that he was unable to make up for the missed ones, he could give Fidyā.

CUPPING, BLOODLETTING AND INJECTIONS

If a person injects something in the body through the veins, or takes blood out for testing diabetes or has Hijāmah (cupping) done on him, in all cases the fast will not break according to the Hanafī research.

Note: Some people say that cupping breaks the fast. They take the Daleel from the Hadīth:

"أفطر الحاجم والمحجوم"

"The cupper and the cupped one have both broken their fast."[126]

Rasūlullāh ﷺ made the above remark when he saw a person cupping another person in Ramadhān while both were fasting.

The Hanafīyah put forward another Hadīth:

ثلاث لا يفطرن الصائم الحجامة والقيء والاحتلام [127]

"Three things do not break the fast. Cupping, vomit and (having a) wet dream."[128]

To reconcile between both Ahādīth, the Hanafīyah say that in the second Hadīth, Rasūlullāh ﷺ is mentioning a general rule. Whereas in the first, he meant to say that they are very close to breaking their fast. Such phrases are normal in the Arabic language.

---

[125] أحكام ص 239

[126] Abū Dāwūd.

[127] رواه أحمد والترمذى

[128] Tirmīdhī, Ahmad.

In order to understand this, we have to look at how they used to cup in those days. They would have a horn of a bull. The sharp end would have a hole, through which the cupper would suck very hard. There was a risk that some blood could end up in his mouth and if he swallowed it, his fast would break.

As for the cupped person, if he fainted or too much blood was extracted, and he became so weak that he had to eat or drink something, his fast would break. This is why Rasūlullāh ﷺ meant to say, "They are very close to breaking their fasts."

INJECTIONS

Hadhrat Muftī Shafī Sahib has written a detailed Fatwā with regards to injections. The Fatwā was then attested, by the likes of Hadhrat Maulānā Hussain Ahmed Madanī and Hadhrat Maulānā Ashraf Alī Thānwī. The reality is that whatever is inserted into the body through injection, travels through the veins before it reaches the heart, brain or stomach. The passage it travels through is not taken as a direct one. [129]

Many examples can be found for this, in the work of the Fuqahā, where they deduce that the fast is not broken when something does not reach inside directly.

They say that injury is of two types:

[1] Aammah [آمّة]
[2] Jaa'ifah [جائفة]

Aammah is a deep injury, which reaches the roots of the brain. When medicine is applied, it goes inside directly. Jaa'ifah is a deep injury that affects the abdomen. Any medicine administered there, reaches the stomach. Since they both reach inside directly, they break the fast.

As for the other injuries like on the thigh, shin, arm etc. any medicine applied there doesn't reach the stomach directly. Even though the effects can

[129] منفذ اصلی

reach the stomach at some level, the Fuqahā state that this does not invalidate the fast. [130]

Muftī Shafī Sahib ؒ writes, it is very clear that injections did not exist in the time of Rasūlullāh ﷺ nor during the times of the A'imā Mujtahideen. Therefore, no one can produce a Hadīth or any quote of the A'imā with regards to the injection Mas'ala. We will have to analyse it with some general principles and similarities.

We can take the Mas'ala from a snake or scorpion bite. The venom penetrates into the body. Most times, snake poison affects the brain and kills. Wasp bites swell the part which was bitten, which means that some foreign body has entered inside. However, no Faqeeh in the world has said that this invalidates the fast. They all say that it should be treated, but the fast will be ok, as long as nothing is consumed orally to treat the bite.

Injections were only invented after experiencing the effects of insect bites. i.e. that the bites had an immediate effect on the body, so injections should also work in the same way, in the sense that the medicine would immediately affect the body, rather than traveling through the stomach and blood system which would require some time.

When we carefully study the wordings of Badaa'ius Sanaa'i regarding the reasons snake and insect bites don't break the fast, we understand that when something enters the human body, it does not instantly break the fast. There are two conditions attached to it:

[1] It should reach the inside of the stomach or into the brain.

[2] It should reach there through a direct passage. [131] (This is why if a stroke patient has a tube inserted into his throat and liquid food goes directly to his stomach, it invalidates the fast).

With the case of an injection, no doubt the effects reach the whole body, however, this is not through منفذ أصلى (a direct, original passage). We see in

---

[130] Masā'il Pg.136. Hidāyah Pg.200.

[131] منفذ أصلى

hot seasons people bathe with cold water. The cold effects go inside the body and cool it down just as a chilled drink would cool it. However, this coolness goes through the pores of the skin and not directly to the inside (jawf).

الجواب صحیح مولانا اشرف علی تھانوی، مولانا حسین احمد مدنی، مولانا اصغر حسین، مولانا اعزاز علی

11 ربیع الاول 1350ھ. مسائل روزہ مولانا رفعۃ قاسمی ص 139، 138، 137

ترجمۃ شیخ عبد الرحیم

Similarly, injections take the medicine, glucose, penicillin, insulin etc. through the veins. Glucose energises the body but just energising does not break the fast. Therefore, the conclusion is that injections do not break the fast, unless an injection is administered directly in the stomach or in the brain.

Please note that it would be Makrūh to take glucose injections during the fast because it contradicts the purpose of fasting. Also, it would be preferable to take all injections after Iftaar, during the night. This is because there is some Ikhtilāf (difference of opinion) in the Mas'ala, so Ihtiyāt (caution) would be better. [132]

ACUPUNCTURE

If someone has acupuncture while fasting, his fast will not break. This is because it only affects the skin. Nothing goes into the stomach.

ENDOSCOPY

If a camera was inserted into the back passage for an internal investigation, it would not break the fast if it was dry. However, they normally apply some gel to ease the insertion. In that case, the fast does break. [133]

---

[132] أحكام

[133] احکام ص 250

ANGIOGRAPHY

In an angiography, a dye which shows up on x-ray is introduced into the blood stream. The principals of Fiqh support that it should not break the fast, as nothing directly reaches the digestive system. However, if medication has to be used, it is better to avoid it during the fasting days, unless it is extremely necessary to save one's life.

LAPAROSCOPY

An instrument is inserted through a small incision in the abdomen to examine the abdominal cavity, or to perform operations. Since it enters the abdomen and normally lubricant is applied to the instrument, the fast will break.

Taking biopsies or samples from the liver or the other organs does not break the fast – as long as this is not accompanied by the administration of solutions or other substances. Maulānā Khālid Saifullāh [*Dāmat Barakātuhum*] analyses it with a Mas'ala mentioned by Ibn Nujaym ﵀, that if a person was to tie a piece of meat with a string and lower it down the throat and then pull it back out, this would not break the fast.

ولو شد الطعام بخيط وأرسله فى حلقه وطرف الخيط فى يده لا يفسد الصوم [134]

GASTROSCOPY

This does not break the fast, provided it is not accompanied by the administration of solutions or other substances. However, gastroscopy always needs a local anaesthetic spray for the back of the throat and if this is swallowed, which in nearly all cases it is, then the fast will be broken.

ENDOSCOPY

This could be via mouth which is called gastroscopy or via the anus which is called colonoscopy or sigmoidoscopy. It would normally break the fast.

---

[134] البحر الرائق ص 279 / 2 جديد فقهى مسائل ص 126

NICOTINE PATCHES

If a smoker uses nicotine patches, the fast will not break. This is clear, because they are applied to the skin and there is no direct penetration to the stomach or the brain.

Note: Consult a Muslim physician before taking any of the above tests whilst fasting. If the advice given is that the test is absolutely necessary, then it should take precedence over the fast. If they are not necessary, delay them until after Ramadhan.

KAFFĀRAH

When a fast is deliberately broken, Kaffārah becomes necessary. Kaffārah is to make Qadhā of the broken fast and then fast for two months continuously, without any break in the middle. If one missed a day, he would have to start the two months from the beginning. The only exceptions to this rule are if one is menstruating or in a state of lochia (post-natal bleeding). A menstruating woman must continue to fast after she becomes pure, and she cannot delay the completion of the expiation. If she does delay fasting after becoming pure, then she must restart the 60 days of fasting. If one cannot fast, he may feed 60 Masakeen (poor people) or free one slave.

Some Ulamā (the Salafī scholars) say Kaffārah only becomes necessary by deliberate sexual intercourse. However, the majority of the Ulamā and the Hanafī scholars say that it becomes Wājib by eating or drinking deliberately (without genuine necessity) as well.

If someone broke a few fasts in Ramadhān, does he have to give Kaffārah for every broken fast, or can there be 'Tadakhul' (combining them into one)?

The Salafi scholars say that Kaffārah will have to be given separately for each broken fast. So if one broke five fasts, he will have to give five Kaffārah.

The Hanafī scholars say there will be 'Tadakhul' in Kaffārah. Then, there are three opinions of the Muftiyāne Kirām:

[1] There can be Tadakhul of Kaffārah for one Ramadhān, not two separate ones. [135]

---

[135] Behisti Zewar.

[2] In *Behisti Gohar* it says Tadakhul can be of separate Ramadhān's as well.

[3] In *Ahsan ul Fatāwā* it says that if Kaffārah was due to sexual intercourse, Tadakhul can be for one Ramadhān only. However, if it was due to eating or drinking, Tadakhul can be for various Ramadhāns as well.

[By Sūfī Muftī Tāhir Hafizahullāh]

The following is an extract written by Sister Naielah Ackbarali. It has been included here for the benefit of the reader. May Allāh ﷻ reward her. Āmīn.

WHAT DOES A WOMAN DO IF HER PERIOD STARTS IN RAMADHĀN?

If her menstruation starts in Ramadhān during the night (i.e. any time from the entering of Maghrib to before the entering of Fajr), then she refrains from fasting the following day and for the duration that she is menstruating. [136]

If her menstruation starts in Ramadhān during the day (i.e. any time from the entering of Fajr to the entering of Maghrib), then her fast is vitiated and it does not count. She must make up this day after Ramadhān has ended in a time when she is able. She must refrain from fasting for the duration that she is menstruating. [137]

A menstruating woman can eat and drink during the day in Ramadhān. If she believes that it is unlawful for her to eat or drink, then it is necessary for her to do so as refraining from food or drink with the intention of fasting is unlawful for her. [138]

A menstruating woman should record the number of days she missed while fasting and make them up after Ramadhān ends in a time when she is able. The same rulings apply to a woman in a state of lochia (post-natal bleeding).

---

[136] Hidāyah Hartford, Birgivi's Manual Interpreted.

[137] Shurunbulali, Maraqi al-Falah; Shurunbulali, Imdad al-Fattah; Tahtawi, Hashiyya al-Tahtawi.

[138] Tahtawi, Hashiyya al-Tahtawi; Shurunbulali, Imdad al-Fattah.

WHAT DOES A WOMAN DO IF HER PERIOD ENDS IN RAMADHĀN?

If her menstruation stops in Ramadhān during the night (i.e. any time from the entering of Maghrib to before the entering of Fajr), then she performs a purificatory bath (ghusl), begins her obligatory worship, and she is obliged to fast the following day and the remainder of Ramadhān. [139]

She must make her intention before the Islamic midday. This is providing that she did nothing that would invalidate the fast from the start of Fajr time. The Islamic midday (al-Dahwa al-Kubra) is the half-way point between the entering of Fajr time to the entering of Maghrib time. It does not mean noon, nor does it mean the Zawāl. [140]

For example, if Fajr entered at 5am and Maghrib entered at 5pm, then the Islamic midday would be the halfway point between this 12-hour time span, which is 11am. Thus, in this example, a person would have till before 11am to make the intention.

Note: There are details to this point if her menstruation ends before the menstrual maximum of 10 complete days and the ghusl time finishes within the Fajr time. Please refer to Hidāyah Hartford's 'Birgivi's Manual Interpreted.'

If her menstruation stops in Ramadhān during the day (i.e. any time after the entering of Fajr up to the entering of Maghrib), then she performs a purificatory bath (ghusl), begins her obligatory worship and she acts like a fasting person until the Maghrib time enters due to the sacredness of the month of Ramadhān. [141]

It is necessary for her to abstain from eating and drinking for the remainder of the day. [142]

She is sinful if she does not do so. However, this day of acting like a fasting person does not count as a fast. She must make up this day after Ramadhān has ended in a time when she is able. [143]

---

[139] Hidāyah Hartford, Birgivi's Manual Interpreted.

[140] Mulla Khusru, Durar al-Hikam Sharh Ghurar al-Ahkam; ibn Abidin, Radd al-Muhtar.

[141] Hidayah Hartford, Birgivi's Manual Interpreted.

[142] Shurunbulali, Maraqi al-Falah; Shurunbulali, Imdad al-Fattah.

[143] Ibid.

She is obliged to fast the following day and the remainder of Ramadhān.

A menstruating woman should record the number of days she missed while fasting and make them up after Ramadhān ends in a time when she is able.

The same rulings apply to a woman in a state of lochia (post-natal bleeding).

SALĀHTUT TARĀWĪH

One of the unique features and beauty of Ramadhān is the Salāh of Tarāwīh. It increases the Noor of Ramadhān. It also increases in our hearts, the desire for worship.

It is narrated in Sahīh Ahādīth, that Rasūlullāh ﷺ led the Sahābā in a special Salāh for three nights during Ramadhān. However, observing the great zeal of the Sahābā and their arrival in huge numbers, Rasūlullāh ﷺ stopped this practice. He did not come out of his I'tikāf area and into the Masjid. He then remarked in the morning, "I knew of your presence. What stopped me from leading you was that I feared it would be made compulsory upon you." [144]

Rasūlullāh ﷺ continued to urge the Sahābā to perform extra worship during Ramadhān, e.g. his saying, "One Nafl of Ramadhān is equal to one Fardh in other months, and one Fardh is equal to seventy Fardh in other months." [145]

He also said, "Whoever stands in prayer at night during Ramadhān with faith and sincerity, will have his sins forgiven." [146]

He praised some Sahābā who were praying in congregation behind Ubayy ibn Ka'b ؓ. [147]

This shows that this special prayer, which we name 'Tarāwīh', does have some basis from the prophetic era. Then, in the Siddīqī era and the early Fārūqī era, matters remained the same, i.e. people would pray behind various Ḥuffāẓ of the Qur'ān. It was in Ramadhān 14 AH, that Sayyidunā Umar Farooq ؓ saw people in small groups behind various Ḥuffāẓ, that he thought, "If I

[144] Bukhārī Vol.1 pg.269.

[145] Ibn Khuzaimah.

[146] Bukhārī Vol.1 pg.269.

[147] Bayhaqī Vol.2 pg.697.

were to gather these behind one Imām, it would be more beneficial." He did have evidence from the practice of Rasūlullāh ﷺ, and since Rasūlullāh ﷺ had departed from this world, there was no risk of it being made Fardh, so he got them all together behind one Hāfiz.

He instructed Ubay ibn Kạ'b ؓ to lead the people with twenty rak'āts. Some narrations state that they would pray eight with three witr. However, most riwāyāt state twenty. It is possible that they started with eight, however, since the rak'āts were lengthy, standing was prolonged and hard, Sayyidunā Umar ؓ instructed them to read twenty, so the rak'āts were shortened and standing was eased.

Abdul Azīz ibn Rufay ؒ says, "Ubay Ibn Kạ'b ؓ would lead people in Ramadhān with twenty rak'āts of Tarāwīh, then he would finish with three rak'āts of witr. [148]

Saa'ib Ibn Yazeed ؒ reports that the Sahābā would stand in Ramadhān with twenty rak'āts during the time of Umar ؓ and during the era of Uthmān ؓ. [149]

Yazeed Ibn Roomaan ؒ says, "People would pray twenty-three rak'āts in Ramadhān Mubārak during the Khilāfah of Umar ibn Khattab ؓ. [150]

Abū Abdul Rahman Sulami ؒ says, "Alī ؓ called upon the Ḥuffāẓ and picked from them some who could lead people with twenty rak'āts of Tarāwīh. Then Alī ؓ would lead them in Witr. [151]

One Dhaeef narration from Ibn Abbās ؓ states that it was the practice of Rasūlullāh ﷺ to pray twenty rak'āts in Ramadhān. [152]

Due to the above narrations, the majority of scholars of the Ummah and all of the four great Imams (Abū Hanīfā, Shāfi'ī, Ahmad and Mālik) unanimously declare that Tarāwīh is nothing less than twenty. (Imām Mālik has said in one Qawl (narration) that it is thirty-six). Twenty has been the practice in Haramayn Shareefayn for the last 1400 years. The correct amount of Tarāwīh rak'āts is twenty; hence, one should always pray twenty rak'āts.

---

[148] Ibn Abī Shaybah pg.165 v.2.

[149] Bayhaqi in as Sunan al Kubra pg.699 V.1.

[150] Ibid.

[151] Ibid.

[152] Ibn Abī Shaybah pg.166 V.2, Bayhaqi pg.698 V.2.

Some people say it is eight rak'āts and they bring forth the Hadīth of Ā'ishā ﷺ. However, this is not correct. She is talking about Tahajjud. Tarāwīh and Tahajjud are both totally different Salāhs. One is early in the night whereas the other is in the latter part of the night. She has clearly stated the words, "In Ramadhān and in other months." Only Tahajjud is prayed in the other eleven months.

SOME MASĀ'IL OF TARĀWĪH

The Shar'ịī ruling for Tarāwīh: It is Sunnah Muakkadah to pray twenty rak'āts of Tarāwīh in units of two at a time, for men and for women.

التراويح سنة مؤكدة لمواظبة الخلفاء الراشدين للرجال والنساء اجماعا [153]

REASON FOR NAMING IT TARĀWĪH

Tarāwīh is the plural of Tarwīhah. Tarwīh is from 'Raahah' which means to take a short rest. Since they would pray four rak'āts and then then relax a bit and then another four and so forth, it was given the name Tarāwīh. The name might be new, but the actual Salāh is not new.

TIME OF TARĀWĪH

The time of Tarāwīh is after performing Ishā until Subhe Sadiq. It is not allowed to pray Tarāwīh before Ishā. If someone was late, Ishā had finished and Tarāwīh had started, he must pray Ishā first and then join Tarāwīh. He can't join in the Tarāwīh and say that he will pray Ishā later on.

Witr should be prayed after Tarāwīh. However, if it was prayed after Ishā and before Tarāwīh, it would still be correct.

ووقتها بعد صلاة العشاء إلى الفجر قبل الوتر وبعده على الاصح [154]

---

[153] در مختار ص 429 / 2 طحطاوى على المراقى

[154] در مختار ص 430 / 2

TARĀWĪH IN CONGREGATION

It is Sunnah Alal Kifāyah to perform Tarāwīh in congregation in the Masjid of the local area. If there is no Tarāwīh Jamā'ạh in an area, the whole area will be sinful.

والجماعة فيها سنة على الكفاية فى الأصح فلو تركها اهل المسجد أثموا [155]

INTENTION IN TARĀWĪH

Tarāwīh and the rest of the Sunnahs and Nawāfil can be performed with the simple intention of Salāh. They don't need to be specified. However, caution is in specifying Tarāwīh as Tarāwīh when making intention.

(وَكَفَى مُطْلَقُ نِيَّةِ الصَّلَاةِ) وَإِنْ لَمْ يَقُلْ لِلّٰهِ (لِنَفْلٍ وَسُنَّةٍ) رَاتِبَةٍ
(وَتَرَاوِيْحَ) عَلَى الْمُعْتَمَدِ، إِذْ تَعْيِيْنُهَا بِوُقُوْعِهَا وَقْتَ الشُّرُوْعِ، وَالتَّعْيِيْنُ أَحْوَطُ [156]

KHATM OF QUR'ĀN

Completing one Qur'ān in Tarāwīh is Sunnah. More than once is Mustahabb, desirable.

(وَالْخَتْمُ) مَرَّةً سُنَّةٌ وَمَرَّتَيْنِ فَضِيْلَةٌ وَثَلَاثًا أَفْضَلُ. [157]

KHATM OF QUR'ĀN IN TARĀWĪH

It is Sunnah to complete one Khatm during Tarāwīh. [158]

One may ask, "How can Tarāwīh and Khatm be classed as Sunnah?" The answer is that Sunnah is that act which was practiced upon with punctuality

[155] در مختار ص 431 / 2 عالمجيرى ص 117 / 1

[156] در مختار ص 82 / 2

[157] در مختار ص 433 / 2 عالمجيرى ص 117 / 1

[158] Durr Mukhtar with Shāmī pg.433 V.2.

by either Rasūlullāh ﷺ or by the rightly guided Khulafā e Kiraam. One Hadīth says:

عَلَيْكُمْ بِسُنَّتِي، وَسُنَّةِ الْخُلَفَاءِ الرَّاشِدِيْنَ الْمَهْدِيِّينَ، عَضُّوا عَلَيْهَا بِالنَّوَاجِذِ [159]

"Hold on to my Sunnah and the Sunnah of the rightly guided Khulafā. Bite on to them with your molar teeth." [160]

He didn't say, "Hold on to my Hadīth." So we shouldn't restrict Dalaa'il with Hadīth, by demanding a Hadīth for everything. We have to look at the general Sunnah. He also said:

"اقتدوا باللذين من بعدى من اصحابى ابى بكر وعمر"

"Follow my two companions after me, Abū Bakr and Umar."

And:

"ان الله جعل الحق على لسان عمر وقلبه"

"Allāh has placed Haq upon the heart of Umar رضي الله عنه and his tongue."

He also said that Umar is 'Muhaddath' i.e. 'Mulham', the inspired one. He also said, "If there was to be a prophet after me, it would be Umar رضي الله عنه."

May Allāh ﷻ reward Hadhrat Umar رضي الله عنه who put so much emphasis on completing the Qur'ān that he preserved the Qur'ān by Tarāwīh.

Shaykh Abdul Qādīr Jilānī رحمه الله narrates in '*Ghunya*' that during the Khilāfah of Alī رضي الله عنه, he once passed by a Masjid on the 1st of Ramadhān. He heard the sound of Tilāwah in Tarāwīh. He remarked,

"نوّر الله قبر عمر كما نوّر مساجد الله بالقران"

"May Allāh fill Umar's رضي الله عنه grave with light just as he

---

[159] ابن ماجه

[160] Ibn Mājah.

filled the Masājid with the Noor of Qur'ān!" [161]

The reality is that if there was no Tarāwīh, many Ḥuffāẓ would have forgotten their Qur'ān. Since they have to lead in Tarāwīh, they memorise and go over it every year. In this way, the Qur'ān will remain protected until the Day of Qiyāmah.

Allāh ﷻ chose Umar ؓ to initiate the Sunnah of Tarāwīh in the present manner. Then Uthmān ؓ and Alī ؓ confirmed it. Not only that, all the Sahābā (who were of the best generation) agreed to it. Allāh's ﷻ hand is upon the Jamā'ạh. The Ummah can never collaborate upon error. So, the twenty rak'āts and Khatm of Qur'ān is the proper Sunnah.

If someone leaves after eight rak'āts, he misses out not on two, in fact three Sunnah's:

[1] The Sunnah of performing twenty rak'āts.

[2] The Sunnah of listening to the whole Qur'ān.

[3] The Sunnah of performing Witr with Jamā'ạh, during Ramadhān. Therefore, we should pray full twenty rak'āts Tarāwīh.

Many Masājid have eight Rak'āts only Tarāwīh. In some Masājid, people leave after eight Rak'āts. They go home and watch T.V. until late at night. Many keep gossiping in the parking lodge while those who pray 20 finish and come out. This is all Mahroomi, deprivation. May Allāh ﷻ guide the Ummah.

TWO TARĀWĪH CONGREGATIONS IN ONE MASJID

It would be Makrūh (disliked) to do Jamā'at twice in one Masjid, on one Imām Musallāh.

"ولو صلى التراويح مرتين فى مسجد يكره"

[161] غنيمة الطالبين ص 427

LADIES JAMA'AH OF TARĀWĪH

If ladies were to join in with men in Tarāwīh, there would be no harm. However, if ladies made their own Jamā'ạh with a lady Imām, it would be Makrūh. If they did so, their Imām should not stand ahead of the Saff (row), she should stand in the middle.

قال محمد لا يعجبنا أن تؤم المرأة فان فعلت قامت فى وسط

الصف مع النساء كما فعلت عائشة وهو قول ابى حنيفة الخ. [162]

A HĀFIZ LEADING WOMEN ONLY [WITH NO OTHER MEN BEHIND HIM]

If a Hāfiz led only women in Tarāwīh, it would be necessary to have a Mahram relative of the Imām or his wife among the ladies. Otherwise, it would be Makrūh to lead women only.

ويكره حضورهن الجماعة مطلق على المذهب كما تكره امامة

الرجل لهن فى بيت ليس معهن رجل غيره ولا محرم منه او زوجته [163]

PRAYING TARĀWĪH IN UNITS OF FOUR

If Tarāwīh was prayed in units of four, would it be ok? If one prayed four rak'āts and sat in the middle for Tashahhud, it would be ok. However, if he did not sit in the second Rak'ah, and prayed four all together, the first two rak'āts will be void. Only the last two will be correct. Therefore, whatever Qur'ān was recited in the first two rak'āts will have to be repeated. [164]

The preferred method is to read in twos.

---

[162] كتاب الآثار ص 603 / 1

[163] شامى ص 307 / 2 تحفة ص 86

[164] تحفة ص 86

RESTING AFTER EACH FOUR UNITS OF TARĀWĪH

It is desirable to have a slight pause after every four rak'āts.

ويجلس ندبا بين كل أربعة بقدرها وكذا بين الخامسة والوتر [165]

What should one read in the Tarweehah (the pause after four rak'āts)? There is no special Dhikr to be made during the Waqfa (pause) between every four rak'āts. One has a choice of doing whatever Dhikr comes to his mind. One could recite some Qur'ān, Tasbeeh, Istighfār, Salāt 'Alan Nabī ﷺ etc.

Some Fuqahā have mentioned the following Tasbeeh which one may pray if he wishes:

سُبْحَانَ ذِي الْمُلْكِ وَالْمَلَكُوْتِ، سُبْحَانَ ذِي الْعِزَّةِ وَالْعَظَمَةِ وَالْقُدْرَةِ وَالْكِبْرِيَاءِ وَالْجَبَرُوْتِ، سُبْحَانَ الْمَلِكِ الْحَيِّ الَّذِي لَا يَمُوْتُ، سُبُّوْحٌ قُدُّوْسٌ رَبُّ الْمَلَائِكَةِ وَالرُّوْحِ، لَا إِلَهَ إِلَّا اللهُ نَسْتَغْفِرُ اللهَ، نَسْأَلُكَ الْجَنَّةَ وَنَعُوْذُ بِكَ مِنَ النَّارِ [166]

WITR WITH JAMĀ'ẠH AFTER TARĀWĪH

It is more virtuous to perform Witr Salāh with Jamā'ạh after having performed the Tarāwīh. This is what Sayyidunā Umar ﷺ instructed Sayyidunā Ubay ibn Kạ'b ﷺ to do. The Sahābā practiced on it and it has been the practice of the Salaf-e-Ṣāliḥīn ever since.

وفيه اى رمضان يصلى الوتر وقيامه بها [167]

QADHĀ OF TARĀWĪH

If someone missed Tarāwīh altogether and the time of Ishā also lapsed, there is no Qadhā for Tarāwīh. This is because Tarāwīh is not Fardh, its only Nafl

---

[165] در مختار ص 433 / 2

[166] شامی ص 433 / 2 تحفة ص 87

[167] در مختار ص 437 / 2

(i.e. Sunnah Muakkadah). If someone missed many years of Tarāwīh, he would not have to make up for them.

وَلَا تُقْضَى إِذَا فَاتَتْ أَصْلًا وَلَا وَحْدَهُ فِي الْأَصَحِّ
فَإِنْ قَضَاهَا كَانَتْ نَفْلًا مُسْتَحَبًّا وَلَيْسَ بِتَرَاوِحٍ [168]

ZAKĀT

Zakāt is one of the five pillars of Islam, i.e. it is from the fundamentals of our religion. Giving in charity is a practice widely encouraged in Islam and as such, Shariah has made it necessary upon us to dispense a small amount of our wealth each year for the poor and needy. When a person's wealth reaches a certain amount, his wealth will be zakatable, i.e. he must pay Zakāt (alms/obligatory charity) on it. Sharī'ah does not like to overburden us, so we are only required to pay 2.5% (one fortieth) of our zakātable wealth.

Due to the increased rewards for giving charity in the month of Ramadhān, many people take the opportunity to give their Zakāt in this month. Therefore, we decided to mention a few points regarding Zakāt here.

There are many virtues recorded in the Ahādīth for giving Zakāt. In Hajjatul Wada, Rasūlullāh ﷺ said:

فَقَالَ رَسُوْلُ اللهِ صَلَّى اللهُ عَلَيْهِ وَسَلَّمَ : اعْبُدُوْا رَبَّكُمْ، وَصَلُّوْا خَمْسَكُمْ، وَصُوْمُوا شَهْرَكُمْ، وَأَدُّوا زَكَاةَ أَمْوَالِكُمْ، وَأَطِيْعُوْا ذَا أَمْرِكُمْ؛ تَدْخُلُوْا جَنَّةَ رَبِّكُمْ -

"Rasūlullāh ﷺ said, "Worship your lord, pray your five (daily prayers), fast your month (of Ramadhān), give the Zakāt from your wealth and obey the commands of your leaders, you will enter the Jannah of your Rabb." [169]

---

[168] در مختار ص 431 / 2

[169] Ahmad.

In another place Rasūlullāh ﷺ said:

دَاوُوا مَرْضَاكُمْ بِالصَّدَقَةِ، وَحَصِّنُوْا أَمْوَالَكُمْ بِالزَّكَاةِ ۔

"Cure your sick ones by (giving) charity and protect your wealth by (paying) Zakāt." [170]

As for those who refuse to pay Zakāt, or those who are lazy and negligent when it comes to giving Zakāt, they should be mindful of the severe warnings found in the Ahādīth. In one place, Rasūlullāh ﷺ mentioned:

من اٰتاه الله مالا فلم يؤد زكٰوته مُثِّل له ماله يوم القيامة شجاعا اقرع له زبيبتان يطوقه يوم القيامة ثم يأخذ بلهزمتيه يعني شدقيه ثم يقول انا مالك انا كنزك ثم قرا ولا يحسبن اللذين يبخلون بما اتاهم الله من فضله هو خيرا لهم بل هو شر لهم سيطوقون ما بخلوا به يوم القيامة ۔

"Whoever Allāh has given wealth but doesn't pay Zakāt, his wealth will be transformed on the Day of Judgement into a serpent, bald (due to its toxic venom), with two black spots above its eyes. It will be wrapped around his neck (like a collar) on the Day of Judgement, then the serpent will take hold of him by his cheeks and say, "I am your wealth, I am your (acquired) treasure." Then Rasūlullāh ﷺ recited, "Those who withhold in miserliness what Allāh has given them out of His grace should not take it as good for them. Instead, it is bad for them. They shall be forced, on the Doomsday, to put on what they withheld, as iron-collars round their necks." [171]

NOTE

The next ten [10] or so pages which contain the Masā'il of Zakāt, I'tikāf, Eid-ul-Fitr and Sadaqatul Fitr are all taken from a booklet which our Hazrat

[170] Bayhaqi in Shu'ạbul Imaan.
[171] Bukhārī.

Maulānā Yūsuf Motālā Sahib Nawwarallāhū Marqadahū had prepared to give out to students before they used to leave for the Ramadhān holidays.

Hazrat has compiled them in an extremely beautiful and succinct manner. This is the beauty of the writings of our Akābir.

Some editing was done by our respected Maulānā Zayd Mehtar Hafizahullāh. The Zakat calculation table was also added by Maulānā Zayd.

THE REQUIRED MINIMUM [NISĀB] FOR ONE TO BE LIABLE FOR ZAKĀT

If a person possesses 612.35 grams of silver or 87.479 grams of gold or any currency that equals the value of this amount of gold or silver, and this wealth remains in his possession for a complete year, then on the expiry of this year it will be Wājib on him to give Zakāt for it. However, if his wealth is less than this, Zakāt will not be Wājib. This amount is known as 'Nisāb'. (The grams are taken from the Hadīth of five Uqiya of silver and five Mithqāl of gold).

If a person possesses the Nisāb, i.e. the required minimum (of silver and gold) at the beginning and at the end of the year, Zakāt will be Wājib on him. If his wealth decreased during the course of the year below the level of Nisāb, one will not be absolved of giving one's Zakāt. However, if his entire wealth was destroyed, he won't be responsible for it, because he himself has become a Mustahiq (viable recipient) of Zakāt.

Note: If someone didn't know the end of his Zakāt year (from the day one became the owner of Nisāb) it may be advisable to take the opportunity of Ramadhān and dispense his Zakāt every year in Ramadhan. One has to keep a fixed date for Zakāt and calculate exactly on that date every year.

CONSIDERING DEBTS WHEN CALCULATING ZAKĀT

If a person is in debt, and his debts are equal or more to the total wealth he owns, he will be absolved from paying Zakāt. However, if his debts amassed to less than his overall wealth, then he must subtract the amount he owes from his wealth. Then, if what remains is equal to or more than Nisāb, he must pay Zakāt on that amount.

We often find that people owe thousands upon thousands of pounds due to mortgaging their houses or purchasing cars on finance. First of all, this is Harām. We should not waste our hard-earned wealth in paying interest, while incurring sin at the same time, a major sin.

However, many people ask, if the overall debt is more than the wealth they currently have, will this type of debt be considered when calculating Zakāt? For e.g. If Zayd had £15,000 in the bank but he owed £15,000 over three years due to financing his vehicle, would he still have to pay Zakāt? The answer is that the full amount owed will not be considered at the time of calculating Zakāt. Rather, the amount owed for that month will be subtracted from the full wealth, so, if for example Zayd owed £500 a month, when he calculates his Zakāt, he will subtract £500 from whatever he has in the bank. Thereafter, if what remains reaches the value of Nisāb, he must pay Zakāt on it, i.e. £14,500 in this case. [172]

If someone lent another person money, he will still have to include that amount as part of his wealth when calculating Zakāt. For example, if Zayd lent 10k to an institute, he will have to pay Zakāt on it, even if that amount stays with the borrower for many years. Zayd will have to pay its Zakāt every year. However, if he no longer had any hope of receiving this money back, he will not have to pay Zakāt on it. For example, if the borrower filed for bankruptcy, he will no longer have the means to pay him, thus, one would not count such a loan as part of his wealth when calculating Zakāt.

UPON WHAT IS ZAKĀT OBLIGATORY?

Zakāt is Wājib on all items of wealth, such as jewellery, utensils and ornaments etc. that have been made with gold or silver. This is irrespective of whether these items are in use or not. In other words, Zakāt is Wājib on everything that is made of gold or silver. However, if the combined value of all these items are less than the Nisāb, Zakāt will not be Wājib.

---

[172] Having consulted various Muftiyāne Kiraam, we have come to believe that the most preferred opinion is that 1 year's payment can be subtracted. In this example, if the monthly payment is £500, then from the £15,000, £6000 can be subtracted and Zakāt will be payable on £9000.

If the gold or silver is not pure but has been mixed with another metal, then one will have to check as to which is more in content. If the gold or silver is more, then the rules which are applicable to both will apply here as well. That is, if they equal the Nisāb, Zakāt will be Wājib. If the content of the other metal is more than that of the gold or silver, it will NOT be regarded as gold or silver.

A person does not have the complete Nisāb of gold nor of silver. Instead, he has a bit of gold and a bit of silver. If both are added together and their value equals the Nisāb of gold or silver, Zakāt will be Wājib. But if they do not equal the Nisāb of either gold or silver after adding them together, Zakāt will not be Wājib. If he has any other Zakatable assets, e.g. cash, shares etc, they will of course be added to the gold and silver.

If a person had money equal to the Nisāb, which was over and above his needs, and then before his zakatable year was over, he received an additional amount. This additional amount will not be calculated separately. Instead, it will be added to the original amount and upon the expiry of the year, Zakāt will be Wājib on the entire amount and it will be regarded as if the original amount and the additional amount was in his possession for one full year. For example, if a person sold his house and got £100,000 in his possession one week before Ramadhān (or the due date), he will have to give Zakāt on the whole amount, even if he was intending to purchase another property with that money. If it came to his possession one week after the calculation date, one will not have to include it. This is because he has already calculated and given his Zakāt. If that amount remains with him until the following year, he will have to pay it at that time.

Zakāt is not Wājib on household items such as utensils, pots, big pots, trays, basins, crockery and glassware, the house in which one lives, the clothes which one wears, jewellery made of pearls, etc. This is irrespective of the amount and irrespective of whether they are being used daily or not. However, if they are kept for the purpose of trade, Zakāt will be Wājib on them as well. In short, Zakāt is not Wājib on all items apart from gold and silver if they are not for the purpose of trade. But if they are for trade, Zakāt will be Wājib on them as well. For example, where a person has a business of cutlery, utensils, washing machines, cookers, fridges etc.

If a person owns several homes from which he collects rent. Zakāt is not Wājib on these homes irrespective of their value. Similarly, if a person purchases some utensils and hires them out, Zakāt will not be Wājib on these utensils. In short, by hiring or renting something out, Zakāt does not become Wājib on that thing. However, Zakāt will be Wājib on the rent accumulated at the end of the year. For example, if one accumulated £10,000 rent throughout the year, one will have to give zakat on £10,000.

WHO CAN RECEIVE ZAKĀT?

The person who has very little wealth or has no wealth at all to the extent that he does not have sufficient food for one day is regarded as a poor person. It is permissible to give Zakāt to such a person. It is also permissible for him to accept Zakāt money.

The person who possesses the Nisāb of either gold or silver, or trade goods which equal the Nisāb of either gold or silver is regarded as a rich person in the Sharī'ah. It is not permissible to give Zakāt money to him. Nor is it permissible for him to accept or consume Zakāt money.

The person who has belongings, which are not for trade/business but are over and above his basic needs, is also considered to be a rich person. It is not permissible to give Zakāt money to such a person as well. Although he is regarded as a rich person, Zakāt is not Wājib on him.

A person may not give Zakāt to one's parents, grandparents, great grandparents etc. nor one's children, grandchildren etc. Nor can a person give his Zakāt to his wife. However, it is allowed to give to one's brother, sister, aunt, uncle, cousin, in-laws etc.

It is not permissible to give one's Zakāt to build Masājid or madrassahs etc. similarly, it is not permissible to help with someone's funeral costs, because 'tamleek' (ownership) is necessary for Zakāt to be considered fulfilled. No one is the owner of the Masājid so one cannot give Zakāt money there, and a deceased person cannot become the owner of any property so Zakāt cannot be given there either.

Zakāt Calculation Table		
Assets		Value in GBP
Gold and Silver		
Value of Gold you possess		£
Value of Silver you possess		£
Cash		
Cash at home	Any currency acceptable in the market.	£
Cash in bank accounts	In any type of account	£
Money owed to you		£
Business Assets		
Shares & Stocks	Resale Value	£
Business Goods		£
Total:		£
Liabilities		Value in GBP
Money Owed (Borrowed or Credit)		£
Employees' Salaries		£
Other outgoings due (tax, rent, utilities).		£
Total:		£
Amount eligible for Zakāt:	i.e. Total assets minus liabilities = Amount on which Zakāt is payable	£
Amount you must pay for Zakāt:	i.e. Amount eligible for Zakāt x 0.025	£

I'TIKĀF

The practice of I'tikāf (remaining in seclusion) is a Sunnah that has remained in the Prophets throughout the ages. It is from the noble practices of Ibrāhīm ؑ and many other prophets used to observe it. As stated in the Qur'ān, Hadhrat Mūsā ؑ was also called to mount Toor for an I'tikāf of forty days, and even before receiving Prophethood, Rasūlullāh ﷺ used to spend a lot of time in seclusion in the cave of Hira. Therefore, after receiving Prophethood as well, Rasūlullāh ﷺ used to observe I'tikāf during the last ten days of Ramadhān on a regular basis.

Observing I'tikāf in the last ten days of Ramadhān is Sunnah Muakkadah Alal Kifāyah. i.e. an emphasised Sunnah, which is the duty of the whole community. If no one from the whole community observed I'tikāf in the last ten days of Ramadhān, the whole community will be sinful.

In order for the I'tikāf of a male to be valid, it must be done in a Masjid wherein at least the five daily prayers are prayed with congregation. As for a woman, she may reserve an area in the home as her place of I'tikāf. It is written is Shāmī that it is Makrūh Tanzīhī or Khilāf Awla (contrary to Sunnah) for a woman to go to the Masjid for I'tikāf. [173]

Although it is not permissible to leave the Masjid or place of I'tikāf unnecessarily, one may leave the Masjid to attend Jumu'ah (if it does not take place in the Masjid he is currently in) and to go to the toilet to relive himself or to go for a shower if he had a wet dream.

If there is no one to bring food to the Masjid, one may go home to eat. Similarly, a woman in her I'tikāf may go to the kitchen to prepare her food if there is no one to prepare it for her.

If someone did leave the Masjid unnecessarily, the I'tikāf will be broken, meaning that the Sunnah of the ten-day I'tikāf will not be fulfilled. Even though it would be best to stay in I'tikāf for the remaining days because he had originally made intention to stay for the full ten days, he would only need to do Qadhā (make up) of that day's I'tikāf. If he doesn't stay, he doesn't

---

[173] Shāmī Pg.441 V.2.

need to do Qadhā of the rest of the days that he missed, because each day of I'tikāf is counted separately.

If a woman started her menstruation during I'tikaf, her I'tikaf will be broken. She will only need to do Qadha(with fasting) for one day , 24 hours from sunset to sunset. She does not need to do qadha of the rest of the days.

It is not permissible to have sexual intercourse whilst in I'tikāf, and if one did so, whether it was on purpose or due to forgetfulness, the I'tikāf will be broken.

It is permissible for a businessman to conduct his business from the Masjid during I'tikāf, though he should not bring the actual goods into the Masjid. One may do his work on the computer, provided he does not disturb others and his work is minimized to necessity.

Some people are not able to observe the full ten days of I'tikāf, because they can't get that much time of work. They ask if they are allowed to go to work and then come back to the Masjid in the evening. In such a case, it will be permissible for a person to remain in I'tikāf, though it would not be counted as the Sunnah I'tikāf of ten days. Rather, it would be Nafl I'tikāf.

One should take the opportunity of I'tikāf and spend the time in worship; reciting Qur'ān, Nafl Salāh etc. If someone has missed many Salāh in the past, it is a good time to start making up for those missed prayers. It is usually very difficult to get a whole ten days just for worshipping Allāh ﷻ. Make use of the time and avoid pointless discussions and futile talk.

THE BENEFITS OF I'TIKĀF

Ibn Qudāmah writes in Mukhtaṣar Minhāj al-Qāṣidīn that there are 6 benefits in spending time in solitude:

1) Freedom of worship, and close proximity to Allāh ﷻ the Exalted.

Once a wise man was asked, "What benefit is there for people in asceticism and staying alone?" He replied, "Proximity to Allāh the Exalted."

Uways al-Qaranī ﵀ states, "I could never perceive that a person would recognise his Lord, and then feel closeness with anything else."

The aim of staying in seclusion is Dhikr and Fikr. This is why seclusion is more virtuous than mixing with people, as mixing causes distraction from Dhikr and Fikr.

2) Protecting oneself from sins which could be committed within mixed gatherings.

These sins are of 4 types:

A) Backbiting: When mixing with people, it is bound to happen. Listening to backbite is also a sin. Sometimes it leads to swearing and abuse as well. By seclusion one can train oneself and cure oneself from this evil habit.

B) Riyā: Showing off. When mixing, we tend to do some actions to show people. During seclusion, we get the chance to keep ourselves to ourselves, and learn to hide our good deeds from others. Riyā is a huge sickness and very hard to cure.

C) When mixing, we are required to enjoin good and forbid evil. Yet many times we see wrongs committed, but shy away from saying anything, which is a form of disobedience in itself. By staying in seclusion, one can protect himself from this sin.

D) In free mixing we tend to pick up bad habits from people. The environment is pretty much out of control. Sin is not only made easy, it's made to look good and people are encouraged to sin as much as possible. This is demonic influence. To get away from Shayṭān, we need to sit alone and contemplate over the purpose of life and learn how to behave properly.

3) The third benefit of seclusion is in saving oneself from fitnah, fights, quarrels, and arguments. During times of fitnah, we are told to control our tongues, stay in our homes, and cry over our sins. This is what will purify our hearts and keep us safe.

4) The fourth benefit is in saving oneself from the evils of the community. People are very cunning. They trick you, accuse you, slander you, and backbite you. They make fun of you behind your back.

Staying away from people protects one from these evils. Sayyidunā 'Umar ﵁ states:

الْعُزْلَةُ رَاحَةٌ مِنْ أَخْلاطِ السُّوءِ

"In seclusion there is safety from evil company."

5) The fifth benefit is that when one stays away from people, they lose hope of gain from him and he loses hope of gain from them. People don't pay much attention to those who keep themselves to themselves. They don't invite such people to Walīma, da'wats, functions, etc.

When one keeps mixing with people, he develops a love for the material world and is filled with greed for luxuries and wealth.

By sitting in seclusion, one can lose all these vain hopes and gain some contentment of the heart.

One Ḥadīth states: "Look at those who are below you, not at those who are above you. This will teach you not to belittle Allāh's ﷻ favour upon you."

6) The sixth benefit is saving oneself from socialising with the foolish people within society. There are plenty of them out there. Many are lazy, couch potatoes. They don't do anything good and don't let anyone else do it.

When one is tested by such people, he will definitely get angry at some stage and speak ill of them and insult them in front of others. This leads to deficiency in religion (dīnī nuqṣān). In seclusion there is safety from this. [174]

---

[174] Mukhtaṣar Minhāj al-Qāṣidīn, pp. 89-90

Imām al-Bukhārī states:

لِقَاءُ النَّاسِ لَيْسَ يُفِيدُ شَيْئًا

سِوَى الْهَذَيَانِ مِنْ قِيلٍ وَقَالِ

فَأَقْلِلْ مِنْ لِقَاءِ النَّاسِ إِلَّا

لِأَخْذِ الْعِلْمِ أَوْ إِصْلَاحِ حَالِ

To meet and greet with people bears
No fruit except for raving gossip.
Lessen your share of men's affairs
Beyond repairing state or learning.

جی ڈھونڈتا ہے پھر وہی فرصت کے رات دن

بیٹھا رہوں تصورِ جاناں کیے ہوئے

May Allāh give us the Tawfīq to detach ourselves from this dunyā and attach ourselves with Allāh Most High. Āmīn.

Note: Sunnah I'tikāf of ten days for gents is only in Masājid or where five time's daily ṣalāh is performed. Ladies can perform it at home: Fix one room for 'ịbādāt. Eat there, sleep there, and do all 'ịbādāt there.

One of the reasons for I'tikāf in the last ten days is to search for Laylatul Qadr. So even if you're sleeping in I'tikāf, you will get Laylatul Qadr, Inshāllāh.

Please also note that sexual intercourse breaks I'tikāf, and so does hugging and kissing.

Get to the masjid before Maghrib ṣalāh, make intention of i'tikāf, and remain there until the moon of Eid is sighted.

Keep this humble writer your duās. Allāh give us Tawfīq and accept. Āmīn.

EID UL FITR

HOW TO PREPARE FOR THE END OF RAMADHĀN & HOW TO WELCOME EID

وَلِتُكْمِلُوا الْعِدَّةَ وَلِتُكَبِّرُوا اللّٰهَ عَلٰى مَا هَدٰكُمْ وَلَعَلَّكُمْ تَشْكُرُوْنَ ○

All this is so that you may complete the number (of fasts as prescribed) and proclaim the Takbīr of Allāh for having guided you, and (so) that you may be grateful. [175]

Allāh ﷻ commands that after completing the عدة, we proclaim Takbīr. In the Eid Khuṭbah, Takbīr is proclaimed nine times in the first sermon and seven times in the second.

To worship on the eve of Eid is recommended, for he who worships Allāh ﷻ on the night of Eid, Allāh ﷻ will enable his heart to remain alive, on a day when all other hearts will be dead:

من قامَ ليلتيِ العيدينِ محتسِبًا لله لم يَمُت قلبُه يومَ تموتُ القلوبُ

The example of a dead heart is a heart which fails to recognise the difference between righteousness and sinfulness. The dead heart falls short in hating the sin and the living heart becomes excited in Allāh's ﷻ worship.

The night of Eid is also when Shaytān is released and works his hardest to mislead you and take you away from ṣalāh and tilāwah. You need to pin him down and overpower him.

How do you do this? Beginning with the night of Eid, begin to engage in Tahajjud. Ḥadhrat Shaykh Mujaddid ؒ would say, "The effect of the righteous actions we performed with punctuality in Ramadhān remains throughout the whole year."

---

[175] Qur'ān 2:185.

Pray Tahajjud on the first night of Eid, and then again on the second night, and again on the third. Fight Shayṭān. Allāh ﷻ will make Tahajjud on the fourth night smooth and easy for you, and eventually Shayṭān will have no option but to flee.

Complete all the Sunnah acts of Eid. Make Ghusl, wear nice fresh clothes, apply perfume, use miswāk, and eat an odd number of dates before the Eid prayer. For the ladies at home who do not attend Eid prayer at the masjid, simply follow masjid procedures and pray at the proper time you would offer your Ṣalātul Eid at the masjid. For example, if Ṣalātul Eid is normally at 8:30am and the bayān is at 8:00am, then one should ready himself and sit downstairs at 8:00am and listen to the bayān attentively via receiver. Upon completion of the Bayān & Khuṭbah, one should immediately perform four rak'ah of Ṣalātul Ḍuḥā Nafl and make lots of Takbīr:

وَلِتُكَبِّرُوا اللهَ عَلَىٰ مَا هَدٰكُمْ ۝

...and proclaim the Takbīr of Allāh for having guided you. [176]

الله أكبر الله أكبر لا إله إلا الله، الله أكبر الله أكبر ولله الحمد

Thereafter, Allāh ﷻ immediately states:

وَلَعَلَّكُمْ تَشْكُرُوْنَ ۝

...and (so) that you may be grateful. [177]

This is the first Naṣīḥah.

After Ramadhān, make Shukr, don't suffice with your good deeds and express pride in the Ịbādāt you performed in Ramadhān. Instead show your gratitude to Allāh ﷻ by making Shukr over the fact he enabled you and gave you Tawfīq to worship him.

---

[176] Qur'ān 2:185.

[177] Qur'ān 2:185.

The benefits of Shukr:

(1) Humbleness is created within.
(2) Allāh ﷻ becomes happy.
(3) Increase In blessings, Allāh's ﷻ promise: لَئِن شَكَرْتُمْ لَأَزِيدَنَّكُمْ

Blessings are not restricted to just food and clothes, but also include spiritual blessings such as ṣalāh, tilāwah and dhikr. Making Shukr for food and drink will result in an increase in this blessing. The same is true for spiritual blessings, where demonstrating Shukr in these blessings will result in an increase and steady firm continuance in good actions.

A Ḥadīth in Tabrānī mentions that, "One who has been bestowed with four things has been given from the goodness of this world and the hereafter: (1) A grateful heart, (2) A tongue that remains moist with dhikr, (3) A body that is forbearing upon difficulties, (4) A wife who doesn't betray her husband in his wealth and herself."

If you are given any of these four things, then you have been given from the treasures of this world and next, so make Shukr of Allāh ﷻ upon completion of Ramadhān.

The Second Naṣīḥah is to make Istighfār (Seek forgiveness).

The Salaf Ṣāliḥīn would stamp there good deeds with the stamp of Istighfār. When you make Istighfār after performing righteous deeds, the good deed freezes, sets, becomes Mahfouz. That is why we recite after Salāh:

رَبَّنَا ظَلَمْنَآ اَنْفُسَنَا وَاِنْ لَّمْ تَغْفِرْ لَنَا وَتَرْحَمْنَا لَنَكُوْنَنَّ مِنَ الْخٰسِرِيْنَ ۝ [178]

Therefore, if there is any deficiency in our good deeds, Istighfār heals it.

Allāh's says in regard to those who engage in Tahajjud:

كَانُوْا قَلِيْلًا مِّنَ الَّيْلِ مَا يَهْجَعُوْنَ ۝

[178] Qur'ān 7:23.

وَبِالْاَسْحَارِ هُمْ يَسْتَغْفِرُوْنَ ۝

They used to sleep little in the night;
and in the hours before dawn they used to pray for forgiveness. [179]

Tahajjud in the night and Istighfār during suḥūr. In conclusion, make Istighfār upon the performance of good deeds.

Sayyidunā Abū Hurairah ﷺ would say, "Fasting is a shield for man, if the shield damages then the enemy's attack would penetrate onto the flesh."

Fasting is a shield but it is damaged via sins (especially backbiting). You will continue to weaken the shield, and eventually break it, if you don't heal it with Istighfār.

'Abdullāh b. 'Amr b. al-'Āṣ ﷺ would daily recite at the time of ifṭār:

يا واسع الفضل إغفرلي

اللهم اني اسألك برحمتك التي وسعت كل شيء أن تغفر لي

He kept his fast, but at the same time was making Istighfār and beseeching, "O Allāh, my fast is not worthy of acceptance, forgive me."

Make complete Taubah. No more sinning. When you make Taubah, your previous history of sins gets deleted. Regardless of whether you break your Taubah dozens of times, always make Taubah again. Inshāllāh, Istiqamat (Steadfastness) will come one day.

Hadhrat Shaykh Zakariyyā ﷺ would give Bay'ạh. In earlier times they would refer to Bay'ạh as Taubah. If you really want to maintain the spirituality of Ramadhān, pure and sincere Taubah is necessary.

The Third Naṣīḥah was regarding Duā'. Make lots of Duā' for Istiqamat.

Allāh ﷻ says:

[179] Qur'ān 51:17.

وَإِذَا سَأَلَكَ عِبَادِىْ عَنِّىْ فَإِنِّىْ قَرِيْبٌ ط أُجِيْبُ دَعْوَةَ الدَّاعِ
إِذَا دَعَانِ لا فَلْيَسْتَجِيْبُوْا لِىْ وَلْيُؤْمِنُوْا بِىْ لَعَلَّهُمْ يَرْشُدُوْنَ ○

When My servants ask you about Me, then (tell them that) I am near. I respond to the call of one when he prays to Me; so they should respond to Me, and have faith in Me, so that they may be on the right path. [180]

In a ḥadīth it is mentioned:

ومن أعطى الدعاء أعطي الإجابة

The one bestowed with the capability to engage in Duā',
will be bestowed with acceptance.

SOME RULES REGARDING EID UL FITR

[1] It is obligatory to offer a two Rak'ah prayer on the day of Eid ul Fitr to express gratitude to Allāh ﷻ.

[2] The time of Eid prayer begins when the sun rises one spear high (i.e. approx. 15 minutes after sunrise) and ends at its decline (i.e. noon).

[3] The Eid Khutbā after the Salāh is Sunnah. Listening to it is also Sunnah.

METHOD OF PRAYING EID SALĀH

One should firstly make Niyyah to offer two Rak'ah Wājib Eid ul Fitr Salāh, including six extra Takbīrs (saying Allāhu Akbar).

After the Niyyah, one should say the Takbīr Tahreemah (Allāhu Akbar), fold the hand and recite Thanā [سُبْحَانَكَ اللّٰهُمَّ ...]. Then say Allāhu Akbar thrice, each time raising the hands up to the ears and then dropping them to the

[180] Qur'ān 2:186.

side. After every Takbīr one should wait as much time as it takes to say سُبْحَانَ الله thrice.

After the third Takbīr, one should fold the hands instead of dropping them. Now the Imām should read Ta'awwuz and Bismillāh, and recite Sūrah Fātiha along with another Sūrah. The Muqtadīs will remain silent as usual.

After reciting the Sūrahs and performing Rukū' and Sujood, the Imām should stand and recite Sūrah Fātiha and another Sūrah in the second Rak'ah. Then, he will say Takbīr thrice as before. However, this time, after the third Takbīr, the hands will not be folded. Rather, they will be dropped to the side, and Rukū' will be performed after saying the fourth Takbīr.

NOTE

When everyone has prayed Eid Salāh, someone who has missed it cannot pray it alone.

If someone missed the first Rak'ah of the prayer with the Imām when he is making up that Rak'ah at the end, he should first recite the Qir'āt and then do the Takbīrs.

If someone joins the Eid Salāh and the Imām has already said the Takbīrs, he should immediately make Niyyah and say the three Takbīrs. If he joins the Salāh when the Imām is in Rukū' and he strongly believes that he has time to say the Takbīrs and then join the Rukū', he should do so. Otherwise, he should go into Rukū' and say the Takbīrs whilst in Rukū'. He will not raise the hands and he won't have to read the usual Tasbīh of Rukū' (سُبْحَانَ رَبِّيَ الْعَظِيْم). If he was not able to complete the three Takbīrs by the time the Imām rises from Rukū', he too should stand. His remaining Takbīr's are excused.

MASNŪNĀT-E-EID UL FITR [THE SUNNAHS OF EID UL FITR]

[1] Personal elegance and adornment.
[2] Doing Miswaak/cleaning the mouth thoroughly.
[3] Bathing.

[4] Wearing nice clothes.
[5] Applying perfume.
[6] Rising early in the morning.
[7] Going to the Masjid (place of Eid Salāh) early.
[8] Eating something sweet (e.g. dried dates) before going to the Masjid.
[9] Going to the place of Eid Salāh one way and returning a different way.
[10] Going to the place of Eid Salāh on foot.
[11] To softly recite اَللهُ اَكْبَرُ اَللهُ اَكْبَرُ لَا اِلٰهَ اِلَّا اللهُ وَاللهُ اَكْبَرُ اَللهُ اَكْبَرُ وَلِلّٰهِ الحَمْد whilst going to the place of Eid Salāh.

SADAQAH-E-FITR

It is obligatory (Wājib) for a person to pay Sadaqah-e-Fitr if his property meets the minimum requirement for the imposition of Zakāt (Nisāb), after excluding the essential things, even if he hasn't been in possession of the property for a full year.

On the day of Eid ul Fitr, if one possesses Nisāb, he must pay Sadaqah-e-Fitr. The passing of a whole year is not a condition of Sadaqah-e-Fitr. This is the difference between Zakāt and Sadaqah-e-Fitr.

It is obligatory for a person to pay Sadaqah-e-Fitr for himself and his minor (non Bāligh) children. If the minor children are wealthy, then it is essential to pay from their property and there is no compulsion on the father to pay.

Sadaqah-e-Fitr becomes obligatory at Subhe Sadiq on Eid day. It is therefore not binding on a child born after Subhe Sadiq or a man who dies before Subhe Sadiq.

QUANTITY OF SADAQAH-E-FITR

The required quantity of Sadaqah-e-Fitr is 1.661kg of wheat or wheat flour, but as a precaution one should give more. If one gives barely or barley flour, it should be twice as much as the wheat.

If someone offers some grain other than wheat and barley, then it is according to the price. The price of that grain should match the value of the required quantity of wheat or barley. It would be better just to give the price of wheat or barley.

If someone didn't pay Sadaqah-e-Fitr on Eid day like he was supposed to, it will not be forgiven. It is necessary to pay it afterwards.

A GUIDE TO

ZAKĀT

Muftī
Mohammed Wahaajuddin bin Mohammed Salauddin

بسم الله الرحمٰن الرحيم

الحمد لله رب العٰلمين والصلاة والسلام على سيد الأنبياء والمرسلين

و على آله وأصحابه أجمعين

One of the fundamental pillars of Islām is zakāt. It is a testament to the deep connection that Muslims have to the dīn of Allāh Taʿālā that on a yearly basis, particularly in Ramadhān, imams and scholars everywhere are inundated with questions pertaining to zakāt. My community is no different. In the past nine years that I have been blessed to be serving the Tawheed Center community, I have received many questions, and many of these questions are frequently repeated. By the grace of Allāh, during the last ten days of Ramadhān, I was able to compile some basic information about zakāt along with frequently asked questions to serve as a quick reference guide. This work is dedicated to my beloved community.

Despite this being a small compilation, several people's contributions were needed to bring this project to its current stage. Special thanks go the following people, in no particular order. To Irfan Shuttari, who is the best friend a scholar could have. May Allāh Taʿālā bless him and his family immensely. May Allāh Taʿālā assist his children who are currently memorizing Qur'ān. To my teacher and mentor Muftī Ahmed Rabbani, who took time out of his extremely busy Ramadhān schedule to look through this, make corrections, and suggest changes/additions. Muftī Sahib is without a doubt one of the most genuinely caring and supportive people I have ever met. He is genuinely happy with others' successes. May Allāh Taʿālā bless him and his family immensely. May He allow us to value him as he deserves to be valued. He is a truly unique gem. To my sister Anaam, who edits everything I write. May Allāh Taʿālā reward her immensely for all the things she does for the dīn and for our family, openly and secretly, and may He put immense barakah in her work. To my mother, who taught me how to write and who took a last look at this work. May Allāh Taʿālā reward her for all her sacrifices and never make her or my father dependent on anyone. And to my wife, who supports me in everything I do. May Allāh Taʿālā give her all the happiness in the world for providing our family so much happiness and stability. May Allāh Taʿālā reward all three of these women for their efforts with the "everlasting Home where no toil or fatigue will touch us" (35:35).

Also, special thanks must be given to Shaykh al-Ḥadīth Haḍrat Mawlānā Abdul Raheem Limbādā دامت برکاتهم for his numerous favours upon me. Haḍrat حفظه الله's belief in me, his du'ās, and his advice to me despite his extremely busy schedule has been a constant source of support and comfort for me over the years. It was Haḍrat who suggested that this work be published, and without hesitation said that he could do it through Tafseer Raheemi. May Allāh Taʿālā always protect him and allow this work and all of his other dīnī khidmāt to be a means of ṣadaqah jāriyah for him.

This work is not "complete" in the sense that I hope to go back and revise, add, and make changes from time to time. If a mistake is found, please bring it to my attention – I will be grateful. May Allāh Taʿālā accept this work and make it a means of benefit.

Muftī Mohammed Wahaajuddin bin Mohammed Salauddin
(May Allāh forgive him and his parents)
Farmington Hills, Michigan
Shawwāl 5, 1442 c/o May 16, 2021

Disclaimer: The views and opinions expressed in this work belong only to the author and are based on his study and research. Every effort has been made to ensure that the correct Sharʿī position is mentioned, but it is possible that other muftīs reach different conclusions. The views and opinions in this work should in no way be assumed to represent or reflect the official positions of Tawheed Center, the author's teachers and associates, or any other institution with which he may be affiliated.

THE IMPORTANCE OF ZAKĀT

Zakāt is one of the five pillars of Islām.[1] Its importance can be gauged from the fact that it is mentioned with ṣalāh – the first thing that a Muslim will be questioned about on the Day of Judgment – 82 times in the Qurān. Linguistically, zakāt has many meanings. These include purity, growth and increase, barakah (blessing), and beautiful praise. All of these meanings apply to the one who gives zakāt. Their wealth will be purified, their wealth will grow and increase, and Allāh Taᶜālā Himself praises the one who gives zakāt. The sharᶜī (legal) definition of zakāt is to give a portion of the wealth specified by the sharīᶜah to a poor, non-Hāshimī Muslim in such a way that the giver is relieved of all benefit and connection from the wealth, for the pleasure of Allāh Taᶜālā.

It is an honor to give zakāt and it should not be looked at or treated as a tax or burden. It is a practical way of expressing our gratitude towards Allāh Taᶜālā for blessing us immensely with more wealth than the vast majority of the world's population. However, in His infinite mercy, Allāh informs us that if we express gratitude, He will increase His favors upon us.

لَئِنْ شَكَرْتُمْ لَأَزِيدَنَّكُمْ (سورة ابراهيم:٧)

"If you are thankful, I will give you more." (14:7)

For doing something we should already being doing, Allāh has promised abundant benefits in this world. One can only imagine what Allāh has in store in the Hereafter for the ones who dutifully discharge their zakāt.

فَلَا تَعْلَمُ نَفْسٌ مَّآ أُخْفِيَ لَهُم مِّن قُرَّةِ أَعْيُنٍ ج جَزَآءًۢ بِمَا كَانُوا۟ يَعْمَلُونَ

(سورة السجدة: ١٧)

"No one knows what delights of the eyes are kept hidden for them as a reward for their deeds." (32:17)

عَنْ أَبِي هُرَيْرَةَ ـ رضى الله عنه ـ عَنِ النَّبِيِّ ﷺ: يَقُولُ الله تَعَالَى أَعْدَدْتُ لِعِبَادِي الصَّالِحِينَ مَا لاَ عَيْنٌ رَأَتْ، وَلاَ أُذُنٌ سَمِعَتْ، وَلاَ خَطَرَ عَلَى قَلْبِ بَشَرٍ، ذُخْرًا، بَلْهَ مَا أُطْلِعْتُمْ عَلَيْهِ ". ثُمَّ قَرَأَ {فَلاَ تَعْلَمُ نَفْسٌ مَا أُخْفِيَ لَهُمْ مِنْ قُرَّةِ أَعْيُنٍ جَزَاءً بِمَا كَانُوا يَعْمَلُونَ} (بخاري)

"Nabī ﷺ said, "Allah said, 'I have prepared for My pious worshipers such things as no eye has ever seen, no ear has ever heard of, and no heart has ever imagined. All that is reserved, in addition to the things you have been informed about." Then he recited: 'No soul knows what is kept hidden (in reserve) for them of joy as a reward for what they used to do.'" (Bukhārī)

WHO HAS TO PAY ZAKĀT?

The dīn of Islām is very practical and takes into consideration the realities of the world in which we live. Each of us needs material wealth to survive. Allāh describes wealth as a means of support for us (4:5). Therefore, zakāt is only obligatory on people who meet certain conditions. The conditions[6] are that a Muslim be:

1. Sane
2. Mature
3. Free
4. In possession of the niṣāb, in excess of debts and essentials, for one Islāmic (lunar) year

WHAT IS THE NIṢĀB?

The niṣāb is a benchmark that is used to determine whether a person is considered self-sufficient or needy.[7] The niṣāb for someone who has gold *only* and no silver or other currency is 87.48 grams (7.5 tolas). The niṣāb for someone who has silver *only* and no gold or other currency is 612.36 grams (52.5 tolas). If a person had only gold *or* silver (not both) and no other currency, they would not have to pay Zakāt unless the amount exceeded the niṣābs stated above. Practically speaking, it is very rare that a person has only gold or silver. Usually they have some gold, some silver, and some cash. Along with these three, sometimes, a person will also have merchandise/inventory. When there is a mix of these things, the gold niṣāb value is used. Since the value is tied to the gold price, it changes. The current value of the niṣāb can be found at darulfiqh.com under the indices section. If the total zakātable assets minus liabilities exceed the value of the niṣāb, and the person is in possession of this amount for one Islāmic year, zakāt is due. When determining if one has the niṣāb for the entire year, only the date of acquiring the niṣāb (zakātable assets minus liabilities) exceed its value and the one-year anniversary (on the Islāmic calendar) of acquisition are considered. It is expected that a person's wealth will fluctuate over the course of the year and at times will go above the niṣāb and other times below. Being in possession of the niṣāb at the two ends of the year signify that a person is self-sufficient and able to sustain themselves despite the ups and downs of life. If a person has more than the niṣāb amount at the end of their zakāt year, they will give zakāt of 2.5% of their entire zakāt asset base, regardless of when individual sums of money were earned. Zakāt is not a tax on *income earned* throughout the year. It is a way of expressing our gratitude to Allāh, purifying our wealth, and helping those less fortunate than us by giving a small portion of what *we have left* at the end of the year.

Note 1: The only thing that is considered is the value of a person's zakāt asset base on their zakāt anniversary date. No consideration is given to sums of money that come into their possession over the course of the year.

> Example 1: Zayd's zakāt anniversary is on Shawwāl 5. On Shawwāl 1, he has £10,000. On Shawwāl 4, the house he was selling closes and £400,000 comes into his account. On Shawwāl 5, he will calculate 2.5% of £410,000.
>
> Example 2: Zayd's zakāt anniversary is on Shawwāl 5. On Shawwāl 1, he has £500,000. On Shawwāl 4, he closes on a house he was buying for £400,000. On Shawwāl 5, he will calculate 2.5% of £100,000.

Note 2: The only exception to Note 1 is if in the middle of the zakāt year, a person loses everything and goes completely bankrupt. In this case, they will wait until they gain the niṣāb again. That date will become the zakāt anniversary, and after one year, if the person is still in possession of niṣāb, zakāt will be due.

ZAKĀTABLE ASSETS & LIABILITIES

ASSETS

The following assets make up most people's zakāt asset base:

- Cash
- Gold
- Silver
- Property for resale/business inventory/merchandise/trade goods
- Stocks: This includes Retirement packages like 401(k)s and IRAs
- Retirement Accounts
- Cryptocurrency
- Debts receivable

Livestock and agricultural produce are considered separately from the things mentioned above. Livestock has its own niṣāb (tables are included) and ʿushr, the zakāt on agricultural produce, has no niṣāb.

LIABILITIES [DEBT]

The only thing that is deducted from one's zakātable assets is debt.

CALCULATING YOUR ZAKĀT ASSET BASE

Assets consist of the sum of:

1. Cash and its equivalents
2. The value of gold and silver (jewellery included)
3. Property for resale/business inventory/merchandise
4. Investments: Stocks, retirement accounts, and other investments

5. Debts receivable

If the sum of these minus debt is more than the niṣāb, and the person has been in possession of the niṣāb for one Islāmic year, zakāt will be due. It will be calculated by taking 2.5% of the zakāt asset base. If the sum of these minus debt is less than the niṣāb, zakāt will not be due.

> Example 1: Zayd comes into possession of the niṣāb on Rajab 10, 1442. On that date, the niṣāb is valued at £4,900. On Rajab 10, 1443, the niṣāb is valued at £5,100 (the pound value fluctuates because it is tied to the gold price).
>
> - After adding up assets and subtracting debt, Zayd has £6,000.
> - He will pay 2.5% of £6,000 in zakāt.
>
> Example 2: Zayd comes into possession of the niṣāb on Rajab 10, 1442. On that date, the niṣāb is valued at £4,900. On Rajab 10, 1443, the niṣāb is valued at £5,100 (the pound value fluctuates because it is tied to the gold price).
>
> - After adding up assets and subtracting debt, Zayd has £5,000.
> - He will not have to pay zakāt. Whenever he comes into possession of the niṣāb again, his zakāt year will begin from then.

Note: The above examples highlight the necessity of having a general idea of what the niṣāb is at all times.

CASH

For zakāt purposes, the following will be totalled:

- Cash on hand
- Personal bank accounts
- Joint accounts
- Foreign currency
- Money in cash accounts such as PayPal, Cash App, and Venmo
- Visa, American Express, MasterCard and other gift cards that are treated the same as cash and can be used anywhere (not restricted to one store or a network of stores)

Note: It is important to distinguish between ownership and permission to use. For a joint account, if a person is able to distinguish how much belongs to them and how much belongs to their spouse, they will use the amount that belongs to them. If it is not possible to determine who contributed how much to the account, the percentage is distributed evenly between the account holders.

> Example 1: There is a single income household where the spouses have a joint bank account, and the husband is the income earner. The wife has no income, but she has jewellery. Every time a paycheck is deposited to the account, it *belongs* to the husband even though the wife has permission to use it however she pleases. When the zakāt anniversary arrives, the husband is responsible for zakāt on the money in the account. The wife is responsible for zakāt on her own jewellery.
>
> Example 2: The scenario is the same as example 1. However, the wife receives a large sum of money as inheritance and deposits it to the account. When the zakāt anniversary arrives, the husband is responsible for zakāt of all of the money in the account except for

the inheritance money. The wife is responsible for zakat on her inheritance money along with zakāt on her jewellery.

Example 3: Both husband and wife work and earn, and both have their own individual accounts along with a joint account. The joint account is used for common expenses and it is difficult to distinguish each spouse's money from the other. In this case, each spouse will be responsible for zakāt on their own account along with 50% of the joint account. If they did not have individual accounts and only had a joint account, both would be responsible for zakāt on 50% of the account.

GOLD AND SILVER

For zakāt purposes, the market value of gold and silver on the day of one's zakāt anniversary are calculated and added to the zakāt asset base. Jewellery is included.

For pieces that are a mix of gold/silver and other stones, ask a jeweller for the amount of gold/silver in the piece, and then calculate the value of the gold or silver and add to the total.

In the rare case that a person has *only* gold or *only* silver, weight will be used rather than the market value.

- The niṣāb for someone who has gold *only*, and no silver or other currency is 87.48 grams (7.5 tolas).
- The niṣāb for someone who has silver *only*, and no gold or other currency is 612.36 grams (52.5 tolas).

Note: If a person has *only* gold *OR only* silver (not both) and no other currency, they would not have to pay zakāt unless the amount in their possession exceeded the niṣābs stated above. Practically speaking, it is very rare that a person has only gold or silver. Usually they have some gold, some silver, and some cash. In that case, the market value of the each is found and then combined.

ZAKĀT ON MERCHANDISE

For zakāt purposes, merchandise/inventory/trade good is any non-monetary item purchased with the intention, *at the time of purchase*, of resale.

- If a person buys something with the intention of resale and then changes his/her mind and decides to keep it for personal use, it is no longer considered a trade good.
- If the product is still being manufactured, zakāt is given on the market value of the raw materials in their current state as raw materials. If it is not possible to find the market price of the raw materials, the cost of the raw materials will be used.
- If the product is finished and ready for sale, zakāt will be given on the market value of the item at the time of calculating zakāt.
- When calculating the amount of zakāt due on merchandise, the market value of the item at the time of one's zakāt anniversary is used. The market value of the item at the time of giving zakāt is not used.
- In the case of a partnership, each partner will calculate the value of their assets within the company.

> Example 1: Zayd purchases a home with the intention of flipping it (fixing and reselling). While he is fixing the home, his zakāt anniversary arrives.

- He will give zakāt on the market value of the home.

> Example 2: Khālid finds an iPhone for a great deal. He decides to try it out and if he doesn't like it, he will sell it to someone else.

- He will not pay zakāt on the value of the phone because his intention at the time of purchase was not exclusively resale.

> Example 3: Bakr purchases a plot of land. He thinks that if he finds a seller who will buy it for a good price, he will sell it to him, and if not, he can keep the land and pass it on to his children.

- The land will not be considered a trade good because he did not purchase it with a firm intention of resale.

> Example 4: ʿAmr sells phones. His zakāt anniversary is on Rajab 10. The market value of his inventory on that day is £5,000. He wants to wait until Ramadhān to pay his zakāt. On the first day of Ramadhān, he decides to actually pay his zakāt. On that day, the value of his merchandise is £6,000.

- He will calculate zakāt on £5,000, because that was the value of his inventory on the day his zakāt became obligatory.

ZAKĀT ON STOCKS

Stocks are purchased with two intentions:

1. Short-term: A person buys and sells stock in the short term for monetary (capital) gain.
2. Long-term investment: The shareholder wishes to be part of the company and partake in its profits by holding on to the stock for a long period of time, usually receiving dividends.

When purchased for short-term (to resell for a quick profit), the entire market value of the stock is added to one's asset base at the time of calculating zakāt.

When purchased as a long-term investment, the percentage of non-zakātable items owned by the company are deducted from the value of the share. For example, a company's stock is valued at £100:

- 10% of its assets are raw material

- 10% is cash
- 10% is produced goods
- 10% are goods that are still being processed
  = 40% total

- 60% of its assets are machinery, tools, land, and vehicles (all of this information can be found on a company's annual report).

Zakāt will only be due on £40. This £40 will be added to the shareholder's asset base at the time of calculating zakāt.

Note: 401(k)s and IRAs are long-term investments. The non-zakātable assets on these can be deducted from zakāt calculations. Further research on this topic is forthcoming.

ZAKĀT ON RETIREMENT ACCOUNTS

In this section, mandatory retirement accounts are discussed. These include cash balance, pensions, and other plans where the company sets aside a portion of the employee's earnings on a mandatory basis. The company then allows interest to accrue on this amount. Sometimes, the company invests the money. The employee has no access to these funds:[15] The withheld salary along with interest is given to the employee at the conclusion of their employment.

It is permissible to keep the sum of the money and interest accrued, as it is considered to be part of one's employment benefits. The fact that the company is terming it interest does not make it ribā according to the sharʿī definition of the word.

- There is no zakāt due on the sum until it is received by the employee, and there is no zakāt due on the years prior to his being given the sum.

Example: ʿUmar worked at a company for 30 years. Every pay period, 5% of his salary was withheld. The company allowed interest on the withheld salary over the course of the years. When ʿUmar retired, his company gave him £500,000 – the amount of salary that was withheld over the years along with interest accrued.

- ʿUmar will not have to pay any zakāt on the £500,000 until his zakāt anniversary arrives. When his zakāt anniversary arrives, he will give zakāt on his asset base. Whatever is remaining of the £500,000 will be included with his other assets.

    - To explain further take the following two scenarios:

1. ʿUmar's zakāt anniversary is on Shawwal 15. He receives the £500,000 in Muḥarram. In Rajab, he purchases a house for £600,000. These £600,000 will not be considered part of his asset base when he calculates his zakāt.

2. ʿUmar's zakāt anniversary is on Shawwal 15. He receives the £500,000 on Shawwal 14. If ʿUmar was already in possession of the niṣāb, this £500,000 will be included in his asset base when he calculates his zakāt the next day, *regardless of the fact that one year did not pass on this specific sum.*

Note: Voluntary retirement plans like 401(k)s and IRAs are treated as long term investments and were discussed in the previous section.

ZAKĀT ON CRYPTOCURRENCY

This is a new and developing topic, and therefore there are varying opinions. Furthermore, as time goes on, it is possible that the understanding of these will change. At the moment, some prominent ʿulamā such as Muftī Taqī ʿUthmānī حفظه الله have experienced doubts about the permissibility of cryptocurrency trading, at least in its current form. The goal here is not to state whether or not it is permissible. Rather, one should consult a local muftī and if they are of the opinion that it is permissible, then the following rules will apply.

- Those crypto assets that are purchased with the intention of resale take the ruling of merchandise. Zakāt is due on the value of the asset on the day of one's zakāt anniversary.
- Those cryptocurrencies that are treated as currencies in the real world (you can actually purchase things with them like Bitcoin) are treated as currency and are thus zakātable.
- Platform tokens that are purchased with the intention to use within its platform and not to be resold are not zakātable.

DEBTS RECEIVABLE

Debts receivable are divided into three types:

1. A strong debt: A debt for merchandise. Loaned cash would also fall under this category.
2. A weak debt: A debt for something unearned, such as inheritance, or for something that is not a tangible asset, such as mahr or what is paid for khul'ah. Wages that have been earned but not yet received also fall under this category.
3. An intermediate debt: A debt for non-trade (merchandise) goods such as clothing for personal use.

For the one owed the debt, zakāt is due on number 1 (strong debt) on the person's zakāt anniversary, regardless of whether or not possession has been taken of the money. For numbers 2 and 3, zakāt will not actually be due until possession is taken of the money owed.

Furthermore, a strong debt will be divided into two types:

1. The debtor acknowledges the debt and the lender (one calculating their zakāt) believes they will receive their money back. In this case, zakāt must be calculated on the loaned amount every year.

   - Example: Zayd loans Bakr £10,000 to be paid back in 5 years. Each year, Zayd will add the £10,000 he is owed by Bakr to his asset base (or, in the case that it was partially paid back, whatever the balance of the loan is). He will pay the £250 (2.5% of 10,000) owed on this loaned amount yearly along with the rest of his zakāt.

Note: If the amount is large and it is difficult for the lender to pay its zakāt immediately, it can be paid once the money is received. In the example above, if Zayd was unable to pay £250 yearly, he could pay £1,250 (five years' worth of zakāt) when Bakr pays him back. However, it is better to pay the zakāt on a yearly basis.

2. The debtor does not acknowledge the debt and the one paying zakāt does not have any reasonable hope that they will get their money back. In this case, the money is considered lost and is not added to the asset base.

This is a common scenario, so consider the following three examples. In all of the examples, Aḥmad loans his cousin £50,000 to be paid back in 5 years:

- Example 1: After a few years, or after the loan is due (5 years), Aḥmad's cousin denies that he owes him at all.
    - No zakāt will be due on the £50,000.

- Example 2: After a few years, or after the loan is due (5 years), Aḥmad's cousin insists that he only owes him £20,000.
    - After his cousin claims that he only owes £20,000, zakāt will only be due on £20,000.

- Example 3: Seven years have passed and Aḥmad's cousin has made no mention of the amount due. Because his cousin is older than him, Aḥmad cannot directly ask him for his money back. He hints at it from time to time but receives no response from his cousin.
    - No zakāt will be due on the £50,000. If his cousin does pay him back later, zakāt will not be due on previous years.

LIABILITIES

The only thing that is deducted from one's zakātable assets is debt. There are two types of debt:

1. Long-term debt: This debt spans over a number of years. The amount one needs to pay within one year can be deducted from assets.
2. Short-term debt: Liabilities that need to be paid within a year. These will always be deducted from your assets.

The following debts can be deducted from your asset base:

- Outstanding (not future) basic living expenses which have not yet been paid for:
    - Utility Bills
    - Medical bills (the portion that is due within one year if it is a large amount and there is a payment plan).
- Housing expenses: One year worth of mortgage and rent (when a lease is signed) can be deducted.
- Items purchased on credit: You have taken receipt of goods but not yet paid for them.
- Outstanding salaries and service fees.
- Unpaid dowry to one's wife: Assuming one intends to pay this during the coming year.
- Personal loans: The portion that needs to be repaid within a year.
- Commercial loans: Only one year worth of payments can be deducted.

CALCULATING YOUR ZAKĀT ASSET BASE:

SUMMARY

The following formula will be used to determine one's zakāt asset base:
(Cash in personal bank accounts + Cash on hand + foreign currency + money in cash accounts/apps + gift cards that are treated as cash + your share of a joint account + the value of gold and silver + retirement accounts [after

consulting with a muftī] + the value of merchandise + the value of stocks + the value of cryptocurrencies + debts receivable)

MINUS

(Outstanding bills + credit balances + outstanding salaries and service fees + dowry to be paid within the year + personal loans due within a year + one year worth of commercial loans)
= Zakāt Base: If this amount exceeds the gold niṣāb*, zakāt is due on 2.5% of the total.

Note: Zakāt can be given in cash and in-kind. This means other items whose value equals the amount of zakāt due can be given.

The condition is that in-kind donations be such that the recipient is given full ownership of the item. The value of the item on the day of one's zakāt anniversary is taken into consideration. If the value of the in-kind donation does not equal the value of the zakāt due on the person, its value will be deducted from the total zakāt owed, and the remainder will remain due.

Some examples of in-kind donations are purchasing textbooks for poor students, giving clothing, or building a home for a zakāt eligible recipient and then making them the full owner of it.

* This Zakat section was originally written for an American audience, and for this reason, the gold niṣāb was mentioned. Reliable ʿulamā including the American Fiqh Academy have given fatwā that in America, due to several circumstances, the gold niṣāb should be used, even though it is higher than the silver niṣāb. Their fatwā can be found at fiqhacademy.com/res04. Also, refer to Fatāwā Dār al-ʿUlūm Zakarīyyā, Volume 3, Page 113: دور جدید میں ثمن عرفی کے لئے معیار نصاب کا حکم and Jadīd Fiqhī Masā'il, Volume 2, Pages 102-103. However, the predominant opinion in many countries is that the silver niṣāb should be used. For this reason, please refer to a local muftī for guidance.

WHO CAN BE GIVEN ZAKĀT ?

The following groups are eligible to be given zakāt funds:

1. A person who does not possess the niṣāb.
2. A poor person who has no wealth at all.
3. A slave working to free himself.
4. A person in debt - the debts are enough that when deducted from his assets, he does not possess the niṣāb.
5. A soldier cut off from his troop or a pilgrim cut off from his group.
6. A traveler who possesses wealth in his homeland but does not have access to his wealth on the journey.
7. One who works for the state as a zakāt collector.

The following groups are not eligible to receive zakāt funds:

1. Non-Muslims
2. Spouses
3. Ascendents (parents, grandparents) and descendants (children and grandchildren)
4. Hashemites (Syeds) [181]
5. Public works projects - construction
6. Organizations who use the zakāt funds to fund operational expenses, advertising, etc.

FREQUENTLY ASKED QUESTIONS

I have set aside some money for (__________) [Hajj, my child's wedding, to buy a car, to buy a house, for college, and so on]. Do I need to pay zakāt on this amount?

If a person's zakāt anniversary arrives and their assets minus their liabilities exceed the niṣāb on that day, it is obligatory for them to pay 2.5% of the

[181] The traditional opinion is that Syeds are not allowed to receive zakāt. However, there is a difference of opinion in this regard amongst some later scholars. There are some riwāyāhs from Imām Abū Ḥanīfah ﷺ stating this, and Imām Ṭaḥāwī ﷺ was of the opinion that they can receive zakāt. Some other contemporary scholars support this view. For more details, see Fatāwā Dār al-ʿUlūm Zakarīyyā, Volume 3, Pages 229-236.

entire amount as zakāt. The intention of using the money for some other purpose in the future, even if it is a day later, does not exempt it from zakāt.

I received a large sum of money towards the end of my zakāt year (by selling a house or stocks, for example). One year has not passed on this large sum. Is zakāt due on this sum?

Zakāt is not due on each individual dollar or pay check one year after earning it. Rather, it is due when a year passes on the niṣāb. If a person is already in possession of the niṣāb and they receive any sum of money, small or large, through any permissible means, even if involuntary (gift, inheritance), it will be added to their existing asset base. When their zakāt anniversary arrives, and they are in possession of the niṣāb, zakāt will be taken from the entire asset base regardless of when the individual sums were acquired.

Can I give zakāt of things besides cash?

Yes, zakāt can be given in cash and in-kind. The condition is that in-kind donations be such that the recipient is given full ownership of the item. The value of the item on the day of one's zakāt anniversary is taken into consideration. If the value of the in-kind donation does not equal the value of the zakāt due on the person, its value will be deducted from the total zakāt owed, and the remainder will remain due.

Some examples of in-kind donations are to purchase textbooks for poor students, giving clothing, or building a home for a zakāt eligible recipient and then making them the full owner of it.

Which of my close family members can I give zakāt to?

Zakāt cannot be given to one's descendants (children, grandchildren, and so on), ascendents (parents, grandparents, and so on), or spouse. It is permissible, and actually preferable, to give to other zakāt-eligible relatives including siblings, aunts, and uncles. In doing so, there is double reward – fulfilling the responsibility of giving zakāt and maintaining family ties.

Can zakāt be given to organisations?

Zakāt can be given to an organisation on the condition that 100% of the zakāt funds be given to people who zakāt eligible. Zakāt cannot be used for communal projects such as the construction of masjids, orphanages, schools, and hospitals, and they definitely cannot be used for the operational costs of an organisation.

Zakāt is the right of poor Muslims. They must be given full ownership of the money or item given to them in zakāt. We understand that some may have given fatwā that in this day and age, or in the circumstances surrounding the pandemic, that it is permissible to give organisations zakāt funds for their operational costs. However, we stand firm on the stance of our predecessors that this is not permissible. There is great wisdom in keeping zakāt for the use of individuals and not for organisations. If not, the door will be opened for wanton abuse of zakāt funds. The following articles give some examples of these abuses.

Can zakāt be used for humanitarian and relief efforts? For example, to build a hospital or purchase oxygen tanks?

It is extremely noble to assist in humanitarian and relief efforts. However, even the most noble of intentions must be brought in line with Islāmic principles. Zakāt is the right of poor Muslims. They must be given full ownership of the money or item given to them in zakāt. It cannot used for communal projects such as building hospitals, digging wells, or building orphanages – even if the ultimate beneficiaries of these projects are poor Muslims.

In the specific question, oxygen tanks (and ventilators) are the property of the hospital, not the patients they are used on. Therefore, non-zakāt funds should be used to purchase these items.

It should be noted that zakāt can be given in cash and in-kind. Therefore, if medicine is purchased and given to a poor Muslim to use, it would be permissible. Similarly, if oxygen (and not the cylinder) is purchased and given to a hospital to use for a poor Muslim patient, it would be valid.

Can zakāt be used to build a Masjid?

Zakāt is the right of poor Muslims. They must be given full ownership of the money or item given to them in zakāt. It cannot used for a communal project.

If I donate money without intending zakāt and then realise that the person I gave it to was zakāt eligible, can I change my intention so that the money counts as zakāt?

If the sum is still in the possession of the recipient, it is permissible to change the intention to zakāt. However, if the recipient has already spent the money or consumed the product given, the intention cannot be changed to zakāt.

I rent out properties/cars. Do I pay zakāt on the value of the property/car?

Zakāt is not due on these properties or cars. Rather, the income earned through renting these properties/cars out will be added to your existing asset base, and zakāt will be calculated on your zakāt anniversary as usual. Even if these things were purchased with the intention for renting them out initially and selling them after they depreciate, zakāt will not be due on the value of the property or car. The income earned through renting and eventually selling the item will be added to your asset based and calculated as part of zakāt when your zakāt anniversary arrives.

I own a piece of land. Do I need to pay zakāt on its value?

If the land was purchased with the intention of resale, zakāt is due yearly on its value. If it was purchased to build something on, or without a clear intention to keep or sell (it's a good price, let's see what happens), zakāt is not due.

Do children who possess the niṣāb need to give zakāt?

Zakāt is not due on children possessing the niṣāb until they reach puberty.

I have set aside some jewellery for my daughters. Do I need to pay zakāt on it?

It depends on your intention. If it remains in your possession and you intend to give it to your daughter at a later date, you will pay zakāt on it yearly. If you have already intended that the ownership transfer to your daughter, there is no zakāt due on it until she reaches puberty. Thereafter, if the amount exceeds the niṣāb, zakāt will be paid on it yearly.

Do women have to give zakāt on gold and silver jewellery that they wear regularly?

Gold and silver were created for the purpose of being currency, and their default state is to be in circulation, not hoarded. The sharīʿah takes into consideration the need for women to beautify themselves and thus allows gold and silver to be worn as adornment. To make up for them being out of circulation, zakāt is still obligatory on them.

Is there zakāt owed on precious stones?

There is no zakāt due on precious stones unless they were purchased with the intention of resale.

Does the person receiving zakāt have to know that it is zakāt?

As long as the one giving the zakāt has the intention of zakāt, the recipient does not have to know that it is zakāt. They can be told that it is a gift or a loan.

A person owes me money but cannot pay me back. Can I forgive his loan and intend that this counts as my zakāt?

Forgiving his debt alone cannot suffice as your zakāt. This is because the intention of zakāt is necessary at the time of giving the money. However, if despite his best efforts, the person genuinely cannot pay you back, *and they are zakāt eligible*, you can tell them to borrow the money from someone else and that you will take care of his debt to that person. Although he can borrow from anyone, it will be easier if you tell them who to borrow from (in which case that person is your wakīl). They will pay you with the money they borrowed, and then you will pay your wakīl/the one they borrowed from with the money you just received. After you pay their debt (with the amount they gave you), this will count as your zakāt. Two points should be kept in mind:

1. This method can only be used if the person is genuinely unable to pay you back.
2. This method is only valid if he is zakāt eligible. If he is not, your zakāt will not be fulfilled.

I don't know my zakāt anniversary. What should I do?

Try your best to determine your zakāt date. This can be done by looking at bank statements. If despite all efforts, it is not possible, choose a date and calculate your zakāt every Islāmic year thereafter on that date.

Can I choose my zakāt date to be the month of Ramadhān without specifying a date?

Zakāt must be calculated on one specific date. This is exactly one year after a person comes into possession of the niṣāb. An entire month cannot be used as a zakāt date. A person's zakāt asset base can fluctuate vastly within the course of a month. For example, if a person sells a house and the sale is finalized in on the 15th of Ramadhān, they will have hundreds of thousands of pounds more as part of their asset base than they did at the beginning of the month.

Can I pay my zakāt before my zakāt date?

It is permissible to pay zakāt in advance. However, zakāt will still be calculated on the date that your zakāt year ends. The amount paid in advance will be subtracted from the amount due. If there is any balance, it needs to be paid.

Can I split my zakāt amongst multiple people?

Yes, it is permissible to give zakāt to multiple people. It is also permissible to give it to just one person.

If my zakāt anniversary is in Rajab, for example, can I wait to pay my zakāt in Ramadhān?

Whenever one's zakāt anniversary arrives, it is best to find an eligible recipient and fulfil the obligation of zakāt then and there. If the delay until

Ramadhān is in anticipation of extra reward, the zakāt can be paid early on a yearly basis. When zakāt is calculated on the zakāt anniversary, the amount paid in Ramadhān will be deducted from the amount due. However, if one does delay until the following Ramadhān, the zakāt will be valid.

Is there zakāt owed on gift cards?

If the gift card is one that is treated as cash and can be used in most places such as a Visa, American Express, or MasterCard gift card, the value will be added to one's zakāt base. If the gift card is restricted to one store (or a network of stores), there is no zakāt on it. It is not the same as currency because there is sometimes an expiry date, it cannot be replaced if lost, it cannot be used outside of the store, and it cannot be exchanged for other currencies.

Can Islāmic schools use zakāt funds for student tuition?

It is permissible to use zakāt funds to pay for the tuition of poor students. However, since tamlīk (giving ownership to the recipient of zakāt) to a *zakāt eligible person* is a condition for its validity, a process must be followed to ensure that this occurs. The school must charge the student tuition at the beginning of the year for the entire year or at the beginning of the month for the entire month. Now, the parents (in most cases unless the student is older) are in debt. If a debtor instructs their creditor to collect the debt from someone else, and that person is paying zakāt, their zakāt will be valid.

The parents (or student depending on the age of the student) can instruct the school to collect the funds to pay the debt they owe for the tuition. Although it is not a condition that the debtor know that their debt was paid with zakāt funds, it is a condition that they be eligible to receive zakāt.

To ensure this, the school can give a form that describes the conditions of zakāt eligibility given to parents whose children will be receiving scholarships. If they meet the conditions mentioned on the form, the parent should mark that they are zakāt eligible and that they give the school permission to use zakāt funds to pay their tuition.

One other point to be kept in mind is that sometimes a parent may not be zakāt eligible due to possessing the niṣāb, but still have difficulty in paying tuition for their children, especially if several are enrolled in the school. If a child has reached puberty and does not possess the niṣāb him/herself, the child is zakāt eligible, even if his/her parents are not. If the child has not reached puberty and their parents are not zakāt eligible, the child will not be zakāt eligible either.

Because it is possible that students may be in need of a scholarship even if they are not zakāt eligible, it is necessary to keep zakāt funds separate from general scholarship/financial assistance funds.

If I do not have to pay zakāt, does that mean I am automatically eligible to receive zakāt?

In terms of determining whether one has reached the niṣāb to pay zakāt, only liquid assets and merchandise are considered. When determining if a person can receive zakāt, other items that are above and beyond necessities of life are taken into consideration. The value of these things is also added to one's asset base and if they exceed the niṣāb, one is not eligible to receive zakāt.

Rather than paying zakāt all at once, can I pay it in instalments?

It is better to pay one's zakāt as soon as possible, but sometimes the situation demands otherwise. It is permissible to pay zakāt in instalments.

If I pay more zakāt than is actually due, will I apply it to the next year's zakāt?

If one pays more in zakāt than is due upon him/her, the extra amount can be applied to the next year's zakāt balance.

I pay Zakāt for myself and my wife. Every month I take a small amount and distribute it. Upon the completion of the year, I do maths, and adjust whatever portion if not paid by then for my wife and myself. My question is that during the monthly payment, do I need to make niyyat for zakāt payment for my wife and my self separately. Currently what I'm doing is I take out 'X' amount from my earnings, and pay for Zakāt to multiple individuals, without making any distinction that this person 'A' is getting zakāt from me and that person 'B' is getting zakāt from my wife. I only make

sure that the receiver of the money is entitled for Zakāt. Later at the completion of the year, I calculate my wife's and my zakāt, and whatever is already paid, subtract it from the total amount due....and release the remainder. Please advise if I'm doing it correctly.

Prior to addressing the question, an important point regarding zakāt must be clarified. If a husband pays zakāt on behalf of his wife, her zakāt will be valid only if she instructs or gives permission to her husband to do so. This instruction/permission can be:

1. Specific instruction: The wife tells her husband to pay zakāt on her behalf.

2. General permission: The husband informs her that he will pay zakāt on her behalf and she either agrees or does not stop him from doing so. If this continues for a few years, there is a general understanding that the husband will undertake this role, and permission will not have to be sought annually.

In some cases, a husband decides to undertake the responsibility of paying his wife's zakāt on her behalf but does this without ever informing her. In cases such as divorce or death, the wife may be unaware of whether or not her zakāt obligation was fulfilled in years past.

In principle, when a person appoints a representative (wakīl) to conduct a general transaction, it is necessary for the wakīl to:

1. Specifically intend the transaction to be on behalf one they are representing (muwakkil) or

2. Use the muwakkil's money.

For example, if a person appoints a wakīl to purchase a shirt on their behalf without pointing out a specific shirt, the wakīl must either intend at the time of purchase that the shirt is for the muwakkil or use the muwakkil's money. Intention is necessary because without specification, there is a potential for every shirt the wakīl purchases to either be on behalf of himself or the muwakkil which would lead to conflict. Therefore, in the absence of the two aforementioned factors, the shirt will belong to the wakīl.

We understood from your question that you are voluntarily paying zakāt on behalf of your wife without any contribution from her. If this understanding is correct, neither of the two conditions for the validity of your wife's zakāt were met. At the time of discharging the zakāt, there was no intention for it to be on behalf on your wife, nor had she given you money such that you could have used it, thereby allowing the zakāt to be discharged on her behalf. Instead, all of the zakāt paid in the manner described in the question is considered to be on your behalf.

As a result, you have paid a surplus of zakāt over the years and, because advance zakāt payment is valid, this surplus will be applied to future zakāt years. As a result, you may not be liable to pay zakāt for several years. During this time, you should calculate how much zakāt your wife owed on a yearly basis, add this together, and then begin paying what you would have usually paid for your own zakāt on her behalf.

SMALL BUSINESS FREQUENTLY ASKED QUESTIONS

I own a service-based business. How do I calculate my zakāt?

Since you do not sell merchandise, you will not have a merchandise aspect to your zakāt. The income earned will be added to your zakātable assets. These fluctuate throughout the year. If on your zakāt anniversary, you are in possession (assets minus liabilities) of the niṣāb, you will pay 2.5% of your entire asset base in zakāt.

For example, the niṣāb is £4,000 on Rajab 1 and you have £4,500. Every month, your company generates £5,000 in revenue. From this, £2,000 is spent in operational costs. The remaining £3,000 is added to your original £4,500, but this is what you live off of. On Rajab 1 of the next year, the niṣāb is £5,000 (the value fluctuates because it is related to the price of gold), and after subtracting liabilities, you have £5,200. You will give zakāt of 2.5% of £5,200. If on the other hand you had only £4,900, you will not give zakāt, despite having generated approximately £60,000 in revenue from your business over the past year.

Remember, zakāt is not an income tax. You only give zakāt on your net assets on your zakāt anniversary. The *amount earned* over the course of the year is irrelevant.

I sell digital downloads (ex: software, art prints, workbooks, etc.). Is zakāt owed on them?

Digital downloads will be treated as ijārah – providing a service for a certain wage. There will be no zakāt on the original software or workbook, but the income earned from selling the downloads will be added to your zakātable assets. These fluctuate throughout the year. If on your zakāt anniversary, you are in possession (assets minus liabilities) of the niṣāb, you will pay 2.5% of your entire asset base in zakāt.

How do I calculate zakāt on my inventory? Do I pay based off of how much the product cost me or the retail value?

The retail value (market price) of the inventory is used when calculating zakāt. This amount is added to your other assets and if on your zakāt anniversary, after subtracting liabilities, you are in possession of the nisāb, you will pay 2.5% of the entire asset base in zakāt.

Do I have to pay zakāt on the value of shipping materials?

Typically, companies do not charge their customers for shipping materials. It is considered an overhead expense, and customers are not charged extra for them. In this case, it is considered that the company gifts the shipping materials to the customer. Therefore, it is not a zakātable asset. If you were to charge the customer extra for the packaging, it would then become a zakātable asset because you are selling them.

"Wrapping and packing materials: are not to be included in the valuation of goods for Zakāt if such materials are not prepared for trade separately. Nevertheless, if such materials increase the value of the goods, they should be included."

I own a home bakery. When I purchase general ingredients, such as flour, I use some for my home/family and some for my business. How do I pay zakat on these supplies?

After purchasing the general ingredients, a portion should be set aside for personal use, and the rest should be left for the business. When your zakāt anniversary arrives, zakāt will be paid on the value of the ingredients allocated for the business. The ingredients that were allocated for personal use are not zakātable.

If there is not a physical separation, you should observe your usage every month and estimate what percentage of the ingredients are used for your home/family. On your zakāt anniversary, this amount can be deducted from the ingredients. The remainder will be zakātable.

What do I do in the event that my zakāt owed exceeds the amount of cash I have on hand? It's possible that a company has assets worth £10,000, while only having £500 on hand. How, then, will I pay the full amount of zakāt owed if I am still waiting for my inventory to be sold?

It is necessary to *calculate* the zakāt due each year on your zakāt anniversary. If it is not possible to pay immediately due to unsold inventory, it will be considered a valid excuse. The zakāt should be paid as soon as possible.

I have a partner(s) in my business. How do we pay zakāt individually or jointly?

Each partner is responsible for their own zakāt on the value of the company's merchandise and cash (after deducting liabilities) in proportion to their ownership stake in the company. For example:

- The company's merchandise and cash equals £20,000 and liabilities equal £10,000.
- You have a 60% stake in the company.

- Your partner, Zaynab, owns has a 40% stake in the company.

You will add £6,000 to your zakāt asset base. If the total amount exceeds the niṣāb, you will pay 2.5% of the entire amount as zakāt.

On what supplies is zakāt due? In other words, is zakāt paid on all assets the company owns including machinery, computers, and other tools?

Zakāt is due on merchandise and the raw materials that are used to produce the merchandise. It is not due on computers, hardware, furniture, the building or warehouse your business functions out of, and other assets that are not for sale are not subject to zakāt.

APPENDIX: ZAKĀT ON LIVESTOCK

This section was included for some of our brothers and sisters who have or are planning to open farms to support the ḥalāl meat industry.

ZAKĀT ON CAMELS

Zakāt on camels is divided into three sections. The total from each previous section is included in the total for the new section. As seen in the charts, if there is a smaller number of camels in the herd, sheep are given in zakāt. When there are a larger number of camels, zakāt is given in camels. Based on this, one may conclude that only sheep are given in zakāt in the beginning, and thereafter, only camels. However, in each new section, the counting "restarts." What this means is that every time a new section is begun, it is considered as if one is starting anew, and zakāt is given in the form of sheep.

Section A

Number of Camels	Zakāt Due
1-4	No zakāt due
5-9	1 sheep
10-14	2 sheep
15-19	3 sheep
20-24	4 sheep
25-35	1 one year old camel (بنت مخاض)
36-45	1 two-year old camel (بنت لبون)
46-60	1 three-year old camel (حقة)
61-75	1 four-year old camel (جذعة)
76-90	2 بنت لبون

91-120	2 حقة

Section B: Add two حقة from Section A to the total. Continue counting normally.

Total Number of Camels	Relative Number of Camels	Zakāt Due
125-129	5-9	1 sheep + 2 حقة
130-134	10-14	2 sheep + 2 حقة
135-139	15-19	3 sheep + 2 حقة
140-144	20-24	4 sheep + 2 حقة
145-149	25-29	1 one year old camel (بنت مخاذ)+ 2 حقة
150	30	3 حقة

Section C: Add three حقة from Section B to the total. Continue counting normally.

Total Number of Camels	Relative Number of Camels	Zakāt Due
155-159	5-9	1 sheep + 3 حقة
160-164	10-14	2 sheep + 3 حقة
165-169	15-19	3 sheep + 3 حقة
170-174	20-24	4 sheep + 3 حقة
175-185	25-35	1 one year old camel (بنت مخاذ)+ 3 حقة

186-195	36-45	1 two-year old camel حقة 3+(بنت لبون)
196-200	46-50	4 حقة

- After Section C, for each additional set of 50 camels, the counting should be repeated as it was done in Section C.
- The total zakāt due from the previous sets (5 حقة, 6 حقة, etc.) should be added to the zakāt due on the current set.

ZAKĀT ON COWS

Number of Cows	Zakāt Due
1-29	No zakāt due
30-39	1 one year old cow (تبيع)
40	1 two-year old cow مسنة
41-59	See below
60-69	2 تبيع
70-79	1 تبيع and 1 مسنة
80-89	2 مسنة
90-99	3 تبيع
100-109	2 تبيع and 1 مسنة
110	1 تبيع and 2 مسنة

- Thereafter, for every 30 cows, give 1 تبيع and for every 40 cows, give 1 مسن.

- The gender of the cows does not matter.
- For zakāt on between 40-60 cows, the following formula is used with *n* being the number of cows:
    - 1 مسن + $\frac{n-40}{40}$ x مسن
    - In other words, the price of a fraction of a مسن will be given.

ZAKĀT ON SHEEP

Number of Sheep	Zakāt Due
1-39	No zakāt due
40-120	1 sheep
121-200	2 sheep
201-399	3 sheep
400-499	4 sheep
500-599	5 sheep
600-699	6 sheep

- Continue to give zakāt of 1 sheep for each additional 100 sheep.

(These tables were prepared by Mawlānā Yousuf Ghouse زاده الله علماً نافعاً وعملاً صالحاً مقبولاً, lecturer of Ḥadīth, at DarusSalaam Seminary. They have been included here with some minor changes in format).

ZAKĀT ON HORSES

For the horses that the owner intends to sell, zakāt of one dīnār per horse or 2.5% of the market value on the day of calculating zakāt is due. For those animals that the owner keeps for breeding purposes, the more cautious position would be to pay zakāt of one dīnār per horse or 2.5% of their value as well.